"Zefyr Lisowski has written a poignant, innovative, and urgent blend of memoir and criticism that has replenished my belief in how art and love can save your life—a book that can single-handedly infuse new and unexpected beauty into your favorite films."

—Torrey Peters, author of *Stag Dance* and *Detransition, Baby*

"This lyrical, thoughtful essay collection is as gripping as any horror movie. Zefyr Lisowski's gorgeous prose belongs equally to the canons of memoir and culture writing."

—Rax King, author of *Sloppy* and *Tacky*

"Here Zefyr Lisowski pushes past the easy discursive tropes of horror, trauma, and trans girlhood, finding and naming the messier, lovelier realities hiding behind and within. In so doing, she gives us a book that's somehow both sharp and generous, and that's a joy to read. I'm in awe—an absolute sensation."

—Jeanne Thornton, author of *A/S/L* and *Summer Fun*

"Expansive, skillful, and tender, *Uncanny Valley Girls* made me think in new ways about seemingly familiar stories. Lisowski is an immensely generous writer with an unparalleled eye for the beauty to be found in the macabre."

—Julia Armfield, author of *Private Rites* and *Our Wives Under the Sea*

"In *Uncanny Valley Girls*, Zefyr Lisowski is unafraid to encounter the most monstrous things—the violences of white supremacy, cis-hetero patriarchy, transphobia, ableism, classism—and consider not only their ubiquity, complexity, and nuance, but also how they live, slyly and softly, in each of us. . . . This fearless inquiry is directed at everyone, not least of all the author herself, and yet its militant commitment to insight never feels punitive. In response to the adage, 'the call is coming from inside the house,' Zefyr answers the phone and asks to speak to whoever—whatever—is on the other end of the line."

—Johanna Hedva, author of *How to Tell When We Will Die*

"In *Uncanny Valley Girls*, horror is more than a genre—it is a language, a sensibility, a lifeline, a semaphore between culture and our own grief and pain and longing. In these extraordinary essays, Lisowski reads the entrails of her life like a witch and invites you along for the ride. How could you say no?"

—Carmen Maria Machado, National Book Award Finalist and author of *In the Dream House*

"This sharp, exquisitely layered book is like a slasher film inverted: Lisowski takes a blade to the big feelings art can evoke, and with great care, she does the delicate paring needed to fit criticism to memoir and to interlace thought and emotion. Horror, revulsion, yearning, shame, and harder-to-name feelings resonate across one another, given space to ring out. The movements of the mind at work in *Uncanny Valley Girls* had me hurtling toward Lisowski's incomparable insight, hard-won though the precision work on display here as she pushes to understand a terrifying, lonely, dazzling, and otherwise incomprehensible world."

—Elissa Washuta, author of *White Magic*

UNCANNY VALLEY GIRLS

Also by Zefyr Lisowski

Girl Work: Poems
Blood Box: Poems

UNCANNY VALLEY GIRLS

ESSAYS ON HORROR, SURVIVAL, AND LOVE

ZEFYR LISOWSKI

HARPER ● PERENNIAL

NEW YORK ● LONDON ● TORONTO ● SYDNEY ● NEW DELHI ● AUCKLAND

HARPER 🟢 PERENNIAL

Without limiting the exclusive rights of any author, contributor or the publisher of this publication, any unauthorized use of this publication to train generative artificial intelligence (AI) technologies is expressly prohibited. HarperCollins also exercise their rights under Article 4(3) of the Digital Single Market Directive 2019/790 and expressly reserve this publication from the text and data mining exception.

UNCANNY VALLEY GIRLS. Copyright © 2025 by Zefyr Lisowski. All rights reserved. No part of this book may be used or reproduced in any manner whatsoever without written permission except in the case of brief quotations embodied in critical articles and reviews. For information, address HarperCollins Publishers, 195 Broadway, New York, NY 10007. In Europe, HarperCollins Publishers, Macken House, 39/40 Mayor Street Upper, Dublin 1, D01 C9W8, Ireland.

HarperCollins books may be purchased for educational, business, or sales promotional use. For information, please email the Special Markets Department at SPsales@harpercollins.com.

hc.com

FIRST EDITION

Designed by Jen Overstreet

Library of Congress Cataloging-in-Publication Data has been applied for.

ISBN 978-0-06-341399-3 (pbk.)

Printed in the United States of America

25 26 27 28 29 LBC 5 4 3 2 1

For us.

Gender is the extent we go to in order to be loved.

—**ROBERT GLÜCK,** *MARGERY KEMPE*

I have this hunger. I thought it was for sex, but it's to tear everything to fucking pieces.

—**GINGER FITZGERALD,** *GINGER SNAPS*

Contents

Author's Note   xi

Prelude   1

I.

The Girl, the Well, the Ring   9
Your Swan, My Swan   20
Our Oceans, Ourselves   29
Ghost Face   50

II.

War on Terror   67
Southern Fried   86
Cutting in Miniature   96

III.

Preliminary Materials for a Theory of the Werewolf Girl   111
Devotion   128
Crazy in Love   150
Uncanny Valley of the Dolls   181

Postlude   207

Acknowledgments   213
Sensitive or Triggering Subject Matter   215
References   217

Author's Note

This essay collection is about survival and endurance, and above all lives lived, which necessitates an accounting of the violences endured and enacted during these lives. That said, in each essay—despite the subject matter—I've tried my best to loop toward hope.

If you think you may need it, I've included an appendix on p. 215 summarizing some potentially triggering material. Whomever you are, please take care of yourself as you read.

Lastly, this is a work of nonfiction—meaning that the events and experiences detailed herein have all been faithfully rendered as I remember them to the best of my ability. In some cases, names and identifying characteristics have been changed to protect the privacy of the individuals involved.

Prelude

Preparing to enter the psych ward, my nerves swelled, and all I could think about was you—the you who broke up with me a week ago, the you who I would break up with in seven months, and the you who would visit me two months later. My body ached for you like the surgeon's hand aches for the scalpel, like the butcher knife aches for meat.

In the selfie I took then, my eyes were red from crying. To distract myself, I watched *Scream* on my laptop in the emergency room as I waited to be admitted. It was my go-to comfort movie; at a time where I couldn't feel further from it, it reminded me of home. Throughout the whole period of my confinement, *Scream* and movies like it were how I rerouted my fear into something more manageable. Whenever I'd stare into my reflection in the shatterproof mirror bolted to the wall, I'd tell myself I was scared of a hunting knife piercing through my aorta, not the murkier dangers I feared lurked within myself. Whenever I'd drink—to calm my nerves—the water was the warmth and thickness of blood.

This is a book about horror, real and filmic, which means it must also be a book about love. For those of us who live in power's periphery—trans, disabled, non-white, poor—love happens under violence's shadow. But love also happens despite these violences, not through them: A love preceded and succeeded by separate horrors is no less a love. In fact, you have to have love to begin with in order to fear it being taken away. So when I talk about horror—and about love—I can't not talk about the hurt, or the rapes, or the deaths, or the moments, quivering and dripping blood, before I entered the ward. I can't not talk about the way the scary movies I saw shaped me, and how I bent that shape until it became something new and gleaming. These movies—their alternate hatred and empathy, their pathologized and victimized women, their strength—resonated with me even from a young age, and the fact of that uneasy allegiance scared and nauseated me. I experienced things I couldn't control while watching scary movies, and in the tightening of my chest I felt even more open to the lives these films depicted: Lives like my own.

To watch a scary movie, after all, is to surrender yourself to the impulses of your body—the extremity of shock or fear overriding all other emotions. Through this surrendering, I believe, you open yourself to other experiences more complicated, learn to name the quieter desires peeking through the rough shawl of fear. Besides, repulsion, one of the foremost responses to horror, is mainly a mark of recognition—*I see myself in this, and I'm scared*—and I also believe anything you can see yourself in so intimately can be turned into a kind of care.

People—even people who have not been broken, if such a thing exists—love horror films. People love horror increasingly more every year, in fact; between 2012 and 2021, scary movies went from taking up about 2 percent of the annual American box office to 13 percent, according to a study in the online movie database The Numbers. There's a well-worn pop-science explanation for this rise: Scary movies, we're told, serve as a controlled release for people craving adrenaline, same as roller coasters. The increase in horror's popularity, the argument goes, speaks to the increased need to relieve stress. The genre, scholars say, thrills without threatening. Horror movies conjure fear without the danger concurrent to fear, and in this way present an escape from the quotidian struggles of the viewers' lives. Horror shows lives unlike our own and this is where it gets its strength.

To make this argument, however, is to falsely attest that the lives in horror films *are* unlike our own—and I learned to love through the ways I saw myself reflected, not pushed away. Despite the ghosts or curses or spree killings, scary movies are ultimately about the weight of violence on a life. They're about the ways to keep living despite a whole world that wants you dead and the legacy of that survival, the parts of you that have given up on surviving. They're about moving (or failing to move) toward care despite being irreconcilably hurt. But they aren't escapist, or at least they weren't for me. Like *Scream*, they showed me the possibility of a place filled with beauty and pain in equal measure. They showed me how to identify a hurt before I even knew how to name my own.

Horror, the French feminist psychoanalyst Julia Kristeva writes, is rooted in the truth of our lives. And truth, she says, is a "barren side, without makeup, without seeming, rotten and dead, full of discomfort and sickness." Horror uses the idea of weakness as a cudgel, inverting its terms: The weak, the rotting are actually strong and will overcome us, and through that, fear is generated. Horror, Kristeva argues, is driven by need but unconcerned with propriety, womanly but not always a woman. It's rooted in embracing and rejecting the feminine to equal degrees, and in that sense every horror movie is about girls and what's done to us.

I have lived passionately again and again; I am covered in passion's pockmarks. Horror movies became an obsession because they were about a similar survival in the face of unbearable pain. The girls who survived, and the girls who wielded that pain, bore the same marks I did. As I walked up and down the ward, my own scars hardening and burns beginning to scab across my body, I understood why these movies—good movies and bad movies, schlocky films and petrifying ones—meant so much to me. It's as important to look back and track the hurt, these films tell us, as it is to dream of a more hopeful future. Besides, it's only through tracking back that we can remember the kernels of care that make life and scary films more tolerable, too: A whispered "I love you" between friends, the wind whipping through your hair while biking from party to party in the moonlit night, a day where nothing happens at all.

When Kristeva wrote her 1980 study on horror and abjection, *Powers of Horror*, she was looking to find a way to purify that abjection. That was her language, to purify. Art, she felt, was the most total way to do that, and according to her the purest forms of art made the abject beautiful. Abject art, she argues, is based in death, the root of all horror: Death "purif[ies] us," and in doing so "establishes a secular religion." But to purify is to sanitize, and to sanitize is to exterminate, which brings us back to death all over again, from the other side. Even as she engages with the abject, Kristeva uses the language of eugenics. She views horror from her position on high, looking down from the seat of power.

Because of this, I love her work but know her work will never love me—so I have to find my own way to understand the way death, the uncanny, and the horrifying have shaped our lives. Horror movies are about death, yes—but death is itself about the life lived beforehand, the choices and connections made before an exit, the place before the fear begins. Another word for Kristeva's "sickness," after all, is vulnerability, and vulnerability always lurks beneath the surface of horror, the wound beneath the stitch. Horror movies are about staying alive, and that focus has taught me more about care than anything else.

Through horror, you can see everything in a life: atmosphere and pain and death and above all the desire to keep living. And in who you watch horror with—because few people I know watch scary movies alone—you can see the rest of it, too: the sex and guilt and grief and everything else that goes into loving yourself and others. I thought of each of my past relationships and of the movies we watched and the ways we reached for each other in the things that wounded us. Leatherface sawing through his leg in *The Texas Chain Saw Massacre*, your finger tightening against my pinky on your beat-up couch. A sea of faceless women in *Antichrist*, neither of us touching the other's body yet, the clock almost midnight. For many of these movies, there's nothing scarier than those peripheral to power embracing their own power anyway, queer or trans or othered bodies finding kinship with ourselves. As we watched countless films showing us both as unspeakable monsters and survivors, we felt held by the hatred and power alike. The miraculous thing about a wound, after all, is not its capacity to heal. Many wounds do no such thing. The miracle is our capacity to live and love despite this wounding.

In the psych ward, I walked the halls. I read. And I wrote, transcribing my experience as much as I could. Notebook open, thinking about the relationships, flings, and breakups that brought me there, I scribbled: *This is a story of love. This is also a story of loss*. But I was also thinking about myself; I just couldn't name it yet. I closed the notebook and stepped outside my room to walk the halls again. Above, the fluorescents buzzed, a wasp's nest. "You are safe," I whispered to myself and other new companions there, until it almost felt true. To be afraid is to care, deeply, about whatever you're afraid of; or, to be more succinct, to be afraid is to care. Scary movies, I believe, can teach you how to live. They can show you the lives you've already led. They can promise what a new horizon looks like. They're how I survived.

When I watched *Scream* in the emergency room, I had seen it at least four times already. I'm sure that's part of why I watched it, why it felt like home. Even on the first watch the violences felt familiar, the snark comforting, the characters understandable in their fear. I watched it, and I texted you, who I would break up with soon. *I'm okay*, I said. *I'm glad I'm here*. After the credits started to roll, I closed the laptop, gathered my things and sat down into the wheelchair that was thrust before me, a requirement to enter the ward as a patient. As the elevator took me up, I thumbed over to that text again, drafting a follow-up I would never send. Instead, I paced the halls, white masks flashing behind every corner, every pang toward self-harm another red knife. I was starting to realize that our relationship needed to end, and as I walked, I thought about how much that scared me, too. It stretched out before me like a set of intestines. It left my body like blood.

I don't want to write a life without viscera or rewrite any pain endured as less intense than it was. It would be dishonest to both my life and the lives of those I love. So yes, I was right in the ward. This is a story of loss, and this is also a story of love. In both, the horrors are ceaseless. In fact, it's all the same story. The horrors are how I found myself, so let's begin there. I promise, at the end, it will all shape into care.

I.

She lives in a dark place now.

—AIDAN KELLER, *THE RING*

The Girl, the Well, the Ring

1.

In 2018, when my pain resurfaced, I thought of it as a punishment. At the time, I was working my coffee shop job where after my shift I'd bike home, write, and go out dancing. Nights I didn't go out dancing, I went on dates. Nights I didn't go on dates, I'd break into the big botanic garden at the outskirts of my neighborhood, scrambling over the fence and walking among hydrangeas bright and pale as the moon. My father had just died, and I filled every second of my time with people, drawing goth circles around my eyes in eyeliner, daubing crimson lipstick onto my lips and kissing strangers with abandon.

That summer I did my best to forget my previous history of sickness, an entire childhood in and out of hospitals, which isn't to say I had become healthy. I still passed out in bathrooms, massaged my aching wrists every night, handled fierce and frequent bacterial infections. But for a while, it was manageable; I could tell myself these were anomalies. Then, things got worse. Every part of me hurt for months. The deterioration I dreaded for so long became my routine. And then that routine became my life.

Fear never produces itself on its own. A young sick child, I'd linger in the horror aisles at the local Blockbuster, picking up cassette after cassette. I was built by scary movies, and those scary movies built how I felt about myself. Girls were punished. The disabled were to be feared. Anything gender nonconforming was even scarier. What does it mean as a sick girl to learn again and again that sick girls deserve to be punished? What does it mean as a trans child to only see a film industry's bile spat back at you?

When my sickness returned, I spent days unable to get out of bed. I had vivid nightmares of monstrous women lurching out of televisions or crammed into attics, bones cracking out of place. I had nightmares that I was monstrous, too. I thought these dreams were further punishment, a reflection of who I had become. Now I wonder how much the things that scare us are always trying to form their own community. In the movies I saw, the thing that was scariest was the risk of contamination—which is to say, the spread and survival of things condemned to death. In these sickened villains, I saw a commitment to a shared endurance, and that scared me. In them I saw, but didn't want to see, myself, surrounded by those like me—girls marked by their illness.

If you first identify yourself in a host of ghosts, what does it mean to live despite that? If you grow up disabled and only have hatred surrounding you in every bit of media you consume, what does it take to turn that hatred into an act of care for others who are hated, too?

2.

As a child, no one talked about why *The Ring* was scary, just about it as a state of being. The autumn after the movie came out, all the girls with the same long thin legs as me walked down their streets extra quickly whenever they passed a tree too flaming crimson. That Halloween, white water-stained dresses were everywhere.

In 2002, my body was a mess. I grew up sick in ways that didn't make sense, each day a new physiological surprise. I'd convulse into seizures when I was least expecting it—on runs, in my gym class, at dance parties, at my uncle's funeral, once while urinating in the middle of the night. I had mood swings that would take over my entire day, hiding welling tears through whole periods of school. My wrists and ankles sprained themselves weekly. Maybe this is why it took me so long to see *The Ring*; the fear it held for otherness was too real for me.

In the movie, Samara, the infamous long-haired girl, had a father who called her evil and stomped around the house and a mother who talked endlessly about how much she loved her daughter. In the movie, the girl was locked in a medical treatment facility away from home and then, once released, locked in a little room at the top of her family's barn. Samara stared, unblinking, at the closed-circuit television in the medical facility she was in, and Samara stared, unblinking, at the bottom of the well.

When I say I felt seen by her, I'm not justifying her evil. It's just that when a movie tells you to hate a child again and again and again, there is something else it is telling you to ignore. In this movie, with all its animosity for people like me, I had found a second home.

A point *The Ring* makes inadvertently is how interconnected all monstrosities are. The young dead girl who's the villain is different and sick, so she becomes a recipient of violence—locked up in a barn, surveilled and neglected in the medical facilities that became her other home. And because she's a recipient of violence, she becomes an enactor of violence. It's important to note that the vehicle for her curse, the videotape, is a depiction of her own pain. Only after she's murdered does she start to kill.

In my own life, I've seen unforgivable acts beget themselves again and again. As a child, I was reduced to receiving medical observation at home and beatings at school, beatings I later enacted again on myself and others, and I learned to watch others closely for signs of difference or sickness, too. Similarly, the girl in *The Ring* is domestically confined and abused, so she becomes a horror—a genre that always infects the domestic and, in turn, wreaks its own violence on the bodies in closest proximity.

By the time I did watch the movie, my father had just recovered from his first cancer scare and I was in the middle of several trips of my own into the hospital. It was 2005; I was in the sixth grade. I watched *The Ring* because it scared me, but also because it and its ilk taught me the consequences of acting out. I took notes: The blond woman was short with her ex-lover because he was scummy, and we felt sympathetic. The girl at the bottom of the well looked scary, so it didn't matter how badly she hurt. The stepfather was loud but ultimately not guilty and that made him redeemable. Anyone who looks dissimilar from the norm ultimately becomes a threat. This is what horror movies do, send their coded moral messages to a whole generation.

But in my friends' scramblings over tree stumps pretending they were wells—long hair draped across the face—we ignored the *other* message buried throughout this whole film. Every time we see her, the girl in the well is clearly sick, and no one who purports to care about her cares about this at all. Unless it's used to stoke fear, the girl's sleep disorder, pale skin, dislocated bones, moods, and deep sadnesses are all completely ignored. Instead—living inside a well, twisting her body within a television—her proximity to the grave becomes her sole defining trait.

As a child, I shuffled from doctor to doctor, and each of them ignored me in a different way—because I was femme, because I was sick, because, to some doctors, I appeared healthy and had nothing to worry about. When I turned twelve, my father started training me to run, following along on his bicycle, telling me that if I became strong, I would stop getting ill so often. This extended to boxing lessons in our garage, a small set of weights in my bedroom, a whole regimen to make my body both masculine and healthy, becoming less and less visible to doctors. Under my father's—and the doctor's—guidance, we built muscles on top of broken joints. I ran varsity until years later I got too weak and had to stop. Even today, I sometimes feel the sudden sting of my long-weakened ligaments as I walk.

I've read dozens of books and articles on *The Ring*, trying to make sense of the film's message, and not a single scholar mentions the girl being sick or disabled. No one mentions why she's deemed *bad*, inhuman, because her body refuses to appear like everyone else's—in the well but unwell. Even at the end of the movie, when we see Samara finally in full frame, rotting with water, she's only presented as an object of mourning. Samara Morgan, in *The Ring*, is just a body filtered through the horror or grief on other's faces, self-mediated by others' disgust, barely a girl at all. A cypher, a ghost, primarily—no, only—hated. She is never allowed to be a girl.

3.

Of course, it's not just *The Ring* perpetuating these ideas of sickness as evil or as punishment. It's an entire blood-soaked society.

Pet Sematary—which I watched as a partner fucked me drunk and upside down on Halloween 2015—features Zelda, a woman with spinal meningitis, terrorizing the beautiful blond main character, her sister. Zelda's hair looks dirty, long, stringy and copper; her skin is sallow and pale; her backbone, exposed and fossilized, pokes through a torn nightgown. I paused the movie and rolled them off me. It was 3 a.m. I was still drunk.

As a sick person who doesn't look sick, I see the revolt in this moment as something that is supposed to be aspirational. I am supposed to sympathize with the beautiful woman and hate the sick woman. Indeed, for most people, according to IMDb reviews, the sister is far scarier than the cemetery that brings the dead back to life, or the spirits lurking within the cursed, colonized land.

Inevitably, the trappings of sickness are supposed to be "scary." In *The Ring*, our first glimpse of the dead girl's face is when she's under a doctor's observation, and this is a sign she's bad. Her skin looks anemic, deep circles under the eyes and electrodes taped under her hair. Even as a dead body floating in the well, the girl wears a dress the color of a hospital gown. Sickness transforms us, the movie says, moves us closer to the world of ghosts and further away from something considered human.

When I was in the seventh grade, I took an EEG test to try to find a source for my seizures. Even though my seizures were debilitating, I didn't yet appear disabled. Instead, I was "otherwise normal"—a phrase that appears again and again on diagnostic sheets throughout my life, from appointments seeking to remedy joint troubles to chronic sinus infections to sudden mood shifts to the autism diagnosis that, in the third grade, doctors decided not to record on my chart "to make my life easier."

The test was inconclusive, and we had a hard time scheduling a follow-up appointment after doctors realized the futility of finding one straightforward diagnosis for me. I've heard this story before, too; after resisting medical categorization, people tend to be tossed into two piles: overscrutinized because you're uncurable or abandoned for the same reasons. I was discarded and dismissed and became invisible to those in power. But if that didn't happen, I'd be turned, as sure as Samara and Zelda were, into an object of scorn and fear.

I felt angry being ignored, but at the time I didn't even stop to think how much worse the alternative was. Hospitals are built on anti-sick architectures of thought, but not all sick people are equal in the eyes of the institution. Perhaps I escaped my own pathologization through my affect ("polite," the doctor said once), or perhaps through the invisibility of my disabilities, but I suspect it was mainly through the color of my skin. Existing oppression proliferates.

Before my father died, he spent three months in the ICU. That summer, my whole body freckled with bruises from the twelve-hour bus ride to visit him. Twenty-four-hour care, the hospital told us, was a medical necessity; checking him out and taking him home was impossible. By the end, my father had had multiple strokes. He was resuscitated twice. He was in withdrawal from acute alcoholism. When I visited, the combination of his bodily pain and the wreckage of my childhood led to us barely speaking all day.

During my time in the hospital, I'd ask for blankets to wrap around my body against the shattering AC, pillows to make sitting in the hard hospital chairs easier. I didn't get any of these things. I was angry at the circumstances we both found ourselves in—my lack of accommodations, his abundance and the little good it did. He was dying, but we were both ignored.

This is, among other things, a defense of rage. It has to be. During my father's death, anger was the only thing that could stifle my grief. As we found out later, there was no reason he couldn't have been released. My father was kept in the hospital, it turns out, because it was the easiest and most financially lucrative option. Half the information we got from doctors—prognosis, chance of recovery, his illness's trajectory—was erroneous. In the end, he became what he feared the most: sick. That's the ending for almost everyone who lives long enough.

"I was laughing when my sister finally died," the blond protagonist says in *Pet Sematary*, and everyone rushes to express empathy.

"If you were," her husband adds, "I salute you for it. No one should have to deal with that *thing* in their life."

I can handle the neglect, but it's the cruelty of it all that tips me toward the sick.

The woman in *Pet Sematary* is actually a man (or is played by one), just like Samara in the original Japanese book is—one last irredeemable thing about these movies glommed onto my own identity. In both, the idea of a woman who doesn't match the standards of normal womanhood, an uncanny woman, is a form of sickness, too.

Medical transition, like disability, is viewed by the mainstream as a sensational departure from normalcy. But the two are not the same, and I don't want to talk about my trans body here because my trans body is not what makes me ill. Besides, my trans needs and my other embodied needs are different: My wrist braces and my tuck may both be made from fabric, but they feel completely different against my skin. The insulting thing about these movies is that they don't hold space for the complexity of a body, lumping every form of otherness together into the same mélange. By *The Ring* and *Pet Sematary*'s calculation, what's bubbling through my joints and what's beneath my pants are both equally, and similarly, repugnant.

Here is my life: I was born, according to some, defective. I went to physical and speech therapy. I went to doctor after doctor. By the time I hit undergrad, my defects were all but invisible. Even now that they've resurfaced, I can go day-to-day without displaying a single one. The surprise on people's faces—*but oh, you don't look disabled at all. I would have never known.*

And then in the middle of this, I came out as trans and tried to pass as a woman who is well. I put on makeup and shut my trap and disappeared from record. I wrote "F" on the intake form at an urgent care and had to fabricate an entire history of menses to the nurse practitioner in order to even make my appointment. I don't request accommodations and am hired for jobs without a second glance, working through flare-ups and sick spells all the while. As long as I don't show signs of being disabled or trans, I'm safe. There's a privilege here, but an immense loneliness, too. And while I've finally learned to find myself in the solidarity of being visible, for years I thought I had to stand alone.

There's a whole canon of literature determined to talk about the redemptive qualities of horror as a mode of truth-telling—the feminist or subversive ways they can be a home for marginalized viewers—Carol J. Clover's *Men, Women, and Chainsaws*, Kier-La Janisse's *The House of Psychotic Women*, and more. But while I like these books, that's not what I'm interested in discussing. These movies—with their sick, twisted women and their healthy heroines—hurt me, and I kept watching them. There's nothing redemptive or revolutionary about that. But they were all I had, and so the pain became a home, too. And now, I'm stuck with it all.

4.

When my father died, I spent months unable to watch anything scary at all. Instead, I thought about how to respond to the horror movies that shaped me. Here is a negative representation, so I will show you why it's wrong. Here's an evil girl, so I will show you how she's the hero instead. But this cause-and-effect thinking is a problem by itself, still adhering to the same rotten goalposts. There I was, like a doctor. I set a problem, diagnosed it, and attempted to vanish it. My father was still dead. I was still disabled. Nothing had changed.

So maybe instead the solution is refusing to answer the question asked in the first place. "When you live on an island and catch a cold," a doctor in *The Ring* says, "it's everyone's cold." The doctor says this to excuse her complicity in the girl's murder. She believes the murder serves the good of "everyone." She believes sick people are the vector of infection themselves. I'm bored by the doctor's casual cruelty, but what happens if we ignore her prompt and start sharing space with ourselves instead, the infected? What happens if we make our own island?

In their book *Care Work*, the poet and activist Leah Lakshmi Piepzna-Samarasinha calls disabled people caring for one another together "revolutionary love without charity." I love how this is an argument not for a positive representation of disability to shift the mainstream's paradigm, but for a different paradigm entirely. If there isn't a supremacist culture to view things through, does monstrosity even exist? Certainly, my own life got immeasurably easier once I stopped hiding every affliction and instead began resting with friends.

So instead of challenging these films, maybe the way forward is to acknowledge the gift they give, oblivious in their own framing. What does it mean to "share a cold" instead of shutting it away? I'm inspired by all the small dominions we, the disabled, have, how much has been shared already. Money. GoFundMes. Personal care assistants. Lists of accessible events spaces. Mutual care and love and support. Knowledge is shared openly online and in group texts and over encrypted chats and through webs of in-person and digitized gossip. Disabled people have created a whole wellspring of culture and activism and vitality—and that buried truth is part of what makes us scary to the abled mainstream. Both Samara and Zelda have full interiorities that the movies cannot see—but that shadow of something beyond the protagonists' comprehension is part of what makes them scary. They endure despite those in power wanting them dead. My partner had chronic pain, as well, and as we fucked during *Pet Semetary* that Halloween in 2015, it, too, felt like a kind of love that rejected charity. Sick bodies doing what they do, refusing to be stifled—together—is a radical act.

When I realized I was sick again after my father's death, I didn't get better. I didn't stumble across a cure. I didn't emerge from the other side in a burst of triumph. Instead, I just resumed the treatments I was engaged in earlier. I started wearing wrist braces to sleep in, took herbal supplements. I booked more appointments with massage therapists and Pilates instructors to help manage my body better. I joined support groups and surrounded myself with the brilliant knowledge of those like me. And gradually, I altered my field of comparison, avoiding the trap of thinking I was grotesque or an other—or more accurately, I realized I had always been different. Nothing had been taken from me. It's not that I was uncurable, but rather the idea of a "cure" was proposed by someone who hated my existence in the first place. Slowly, I built a community out of a life, and in that way, I began to heal.

I'm grateful for what I've made. I'm grateful for the anger that propelled this making in the first place. But even still, I have to wonder what my life would be like had I never been exposed to these supremacist messages in the first place.

Here's one last little story.

In *The Ring*, when the girl climbs up the well, her bones cracking out of place, bending behind herself, this is supposed to be a sign she's to be feared and pitied and isn't even human.

When I discovered, suddenly as a child, that I could do the same thing, oh, it felt like freedom.

Your Swan, My Swan

We watch the movie together on New Year's Eve, 2015—or technically New Year's Day, 2016, since we're watching it at 3 a.m. "I'm sorry," you told me at the club, after you found me histrionic in the bathroom stall. "You'll have to sleep on the couch. But I'm happy to host you."

Before we both go to bed, you press play. It's your favorite scary movie—even though I don't, have never found it scary—and you think it would calm me down. You share a small one-bedroom in Bed-Stuy with your other partner—a bedroom that I will move into on my own four and a half years later once the pandemic hits. We have been dating for just seven months and I would do anything to be near you. *Black Swan* starts and soon Nina is squawking like a bird.

In *Black Swan*, Nina, a dancer, hallucinates for the whole film. She's purpled with want, desperate. By the middle of the movie, she conjures up a bruisingly intimate sex scene with her dance partner and competitor, Lily, who throws her to the bed, peels off Nina's jeans and runs her tongue up the inverted seashell of her navel. For most of the movie, Nina is small, helpless, all bound feet and bird bones. But when she comes, she tenses even further, furrows bursting open her face almost completely.

When we first started talking to each other, we were in Asheville, and I was still a scruffy they/them. We met at a friend's poetry reading they threw at their apartment downtown; you were wearing vegan Docs and jeans ripped between your thighs. We both loved *Yeezus* and Edward Said and several months later you recognized me when I dropped off a résumé at the art gallery. After I was hired, I started bringing my lunches to work, even off shifts, because I wanted to be closer to you. We saw each other more and more: riding our mopeds around town to meet each other, crashing events at the private liberal-arts college on a large farm outside town. Three months into knowing each other, I got too drunk at a Halloween party and rushed over as soon as I saw you enter the room, leaving my partner alone by the door to tell you a ghost story. You'd probably already heard me tell it, but I just wanted an excuse to get close. I was in deep.

At the party you leaned in at the right parts of the story and gasped at the others. My costume that year was a sexy cat, so I wore pleather pants and eight nipple pasties dotted down my bare chest. Black and orange streamers dangled everywhere and my two nipples, the real ones, pricked up in the cold. "The cemetery was so scary," I said. "We could tell there was something there that wasn't us."

Horror movies live in the interregnum of the uncanny, a world ripe with anticipation. This is why they are so frightening. They are close enough to unnerve, and like a mirror they reflect us back—distorted into something strange and new. But isn't that love, too? Doesn't everything worth doing change you?

In *Black Swan*, the protagonist dies at the end. Nina dies, the movie suggests, because she can't change while the world around her does. In this way she differs from most horror protagonists, who bend but rarely break to survive a violent world. Personal shibboleths against killing get discarded, shrinking violets turn into hardened women, but they survive despite, or because of, these changes. There's a whole term for it, which the scholar Carol J. Clover coined in a 1987 essay: the final girl, the one who lives because of how she transforms.

I saw myself in these final girls, as we all are taught to as audience members—even if many of us haven't been hardened into killers, haven't learned how to wound others in order to live. But I saw myself beyond that, too. There was a fierceness to my want for them that I was finally starting to understand that night, a girlness twinned to mine. Let me be precise: I was crying in the bathroom because I knew I was trans and didn't know you were, too. More to the point, I knew I had to change my life and didn't know how to include you in it. How could I? My models, in part, were the movies I watched, and I didn't want to bend *or* break, even if the world I was in was killing me. Besides, the world beyond—hormones, surgery, whatever—felt infinite and terrifying in its breadth, too. So, gulping down the cold air, I tried not to imagine either. I was not yet twenty-two. My father hadn't even died yet.

Instead, I thought of you. Our love, I decided on the car ride back to your apartment, was an intense one, one that left marks. Because of this, we needed to stay in it—after all, it had already been seven months of flinging our bodies against each other. That summer, you accidentally broke your ankle while we made out drunk in a stairwell and biked home on a still swelling leg. When I first visited you in New York several months before that, I saw a painting you wanted of the Last Supper in your alleyway and dove through a chain-link fence to get it, tearing up my arm in the process and dripping blood all down your stairway. In the mornings early on in our relationship, we'd untangle from your sheets, necks pocked with hickeys and barely rested from the night before. "I love you," you had said as you rescued me from the bathroom, and it popped out like a marble from your mouth. Neither of us had said it before to each other and its newness ticked through the whole car ride to your apartment, marking the silence before we got home with its constant uneasy metronome.

"When I don't see you, I grow crazy," you had written me several weeks before the New Year. "You're all I think of. You're all I need."

Horror movies present worlds where horrible things happen on top of one another; people die, are psychically and physically mutilated, are abandoned. In presenting the worst possible outcomes for a life, they make our futures feel safer—but by ignoring the potential for growth, the fear beneath still festers. Only certain types of connection are typically shown in a scary movie, after all. Stabbings, failed relationships, jealousy—these movies show intimacies rooted in simple fears, not complex ones. I was afraid of the intensity of our relationship, but I was more afraid of being alone.

A year and a half from now, you'll take the Amtrak down with me to Richmond for my father's funeral, but, for now, it's New Year's Day. We're watching the movie on your couch. "Our new Swan Queen," Lily says to Nina. "You must be so excited. Are you freaking out?" Before the funeral, my hands will be too shaky to apply my eyeliner, so you'll do it for me. We'll snap a photo together in my mother's lavender bathroom; and then we'll go downstairs to the wake. "I'll do anything for you," you'll say, and outside will palm me a rosebud cigarette. As I inhale, the smoke will sting like a kiss. Everyone looks at us: Your fat body and my trans body both harden the gazes of people, and there you'll squeeze my hand three times in quick succession like a blood pressure cuff. At the wake you only leave my side to refill our glasses with tangy G&Ts. You will still tell me you're cis. Later that night you'll want to fuck, and we'll fight, briefly, when I say no.

"She needs love to break the spell," Nina says with wonder about the ballet she's about to dance.

As the movie reels on, this is what I know about our love: It hurts and I want it, and that desire scares me, too. We were friends before we started seeing each other, but really, we knew nothing: not about my moodiness or your spurts of anger, the way we'd both be found and betrayed by our bodies in equal measure. ("Why can't you tell me what you want?" you screamed on your fire escape back in September, Parliament dangling from your fingers, during our first fight.) I didn't yet know about the movies we'd watch together to fill the silence when we didn't speak, or the congregation of tattoos under your clothes that I would talk about when I did talk about how much I desired you. An anglerfish. A giraffe skeleton. A Steinbeck quote across your sternum you got when you were seventeen.

"I'm sorry," I had said on an early date and then we were kicking couch cushions as we took turns going down on each other, my mouth salty and filled with you. Then, I was just starting to learn how often I would apologize or how infrequently you would, the ripe plummy taste of the hair under your arms. I thought I'd find myself through you—even though you later told me you could barely find yourself. Your chronic pain, you said, prevented you from even having the energy to pursue top surgery. "When I get better," you told me, "I'll change my body. For now, I rest."

In *Black Swan*, Nina is crazed with desire to be the only one, the best dancer at the expense of everyone else. She is urged on in this regard by the predatory male director of her dance troupe. She imagines fucking her competitor and this is a way of vanquishing her, too, confronting the jealousy she feels and transfiguring it into pure want. But her goals fail: Throughout the whole film, the main thing you notice is how completely alone she is. Even in her hallucinations she only sees doppelgängers. How sad, to only see yourself when conjuring up what you fear most, to be alone when envisioning danger. We're together, and I'm still trying to hide the aloneness I feel—a kindness to you, a way to prevent my needs from impinging on yours. Unlike Nina, I want us to be more similar and ignore our own differences because of that. The future I would choose and the one you, for now, would not.

Your arm curls over my shoulder. We watch in silence. The clock ticks onward. When you rise from your bedroom in the morning, several hours before I do, you will take a photo of me sprawled unconscious on the couch, hair maned across a pillow, and later that afternoon you will text it to me. I'll still be dreaming of the movie, lost within its own tidal waves of desire and fear. I'll still be thinking of you.

My swan, you'll text, as you send it.

Let me talk about hate, love's cousin. Darren Aronofsky, *Black Swan*'s director, seems to hate the abject and anyone else who death touches.

In his most widely acclaimed movies—i.e., *Requiem for a Dream*, *The Whale*, and *Black Swan*—he picks a different group and shows them living in misery: drug users, fat people, mentally ill women. He refuses to consider them capable of being survivors or holding a complex interiority beyond their own pathologies. He refuses to think of them, it seems, as wholly alive. Indeed, one of the main flaws of *Black Swan* is its inability to consider Nina as a full person, never having a moment of lucidity outside her delusions. When she sees things that aren't there, the movie, lazy and cruel, assumes she'll never know the truth. Intoxicated with her own hysteria, Nina stumbles between emotions with no space for reflection in between. The movie is drunk with hate, refusing to let in anything outside its own worldview. It refuses Nina the category of the human. And because of that, she dies.

I refuse to hold any ideology close that so narrowly envisions a life, believes its destruction is a comfort. I refuse to be horrified by anyone who is like me, or you—living desperately and fully as best as they can. That was what I didn't realize in the bathroom stall: We were more like each other than not, and that still wasn't enough to keep us together in the end. We were scarier in our similarities to each other, not our differences: both ill, both in pain, both not exactly girls when we started to date. I changed in specific ways that you didn't, but that's beside the point: On some level, I knew I was looking in a mirror.

Listen, my moments of greatest abandon have always been followed by realizations of what changes I need to make in my life, whether or not I follow through. Years later, when my father dies, or even after that, when I enter the ward and realize we'll have to break up, I'll see the past and the future alike with more clarity than I ever had. The fact that Nina doesn't have these moments makes her life seem even lonelier and narrower. Her inability to change reaffirms her nearness to death, the cruel disregard Aronofsky seems to hold her in. She has no one to care for her, let alone the capacity to care for others, for herself. In the movie we watched, there was no moving on from the manic highs of an imagined relationship or the warm glow of accomplishment. Instead, there was torment and then the joy of delusion. *Black Swan* doesn't scare me because it doesn't feel real.

As I turn over on the cushions, I wonder what a version of *Black Swan* that held the complexity we were building in our own lives would look like. How would things shift if Nina felt she had the agency to love? Could she survive past the end of the film? Would her relationship to Lily—jealous, paranoid, and one-sided—change as well? I drift asleep on your couch and wonder if you felt scared about where we could go next. I wonder if you wondered what would happen when we sobered up to our own uncanny intimacies, our own barren discomfort.

In the morning as you're about to take the picture of me, I'm facing you, although I mostly slept against the wall then. It's dark still, although starting to get brighter, and you won't need the flash. "I can't be there for you," you'll tell me years later, after I've transitioned and you've stopped. "I need to be present for myself." Your brow will furrow slightly as you say so. We will both be crying. I'll go outside and smoke another herbal cigarette. Nina spinning, by herself, in the practice space for hours. Nina, laughing in the club with Lily during an imagined night out. Your arm around me as we watch, your swan.

Black Swan is a movie about someone whose devotion is so pure it annihilates her. Or rather, *Black Swan* is a movie about someone who is persuaded to believe in an art so pure it can annihilate, and in doing so makes it true. Or, *Black Swan* is a movie about someone who is looking for any excuse to escape herself, so she turns to art instead of love. When Nina dies—because of course she dies—it's in adulation after finishing her performance, and the movie presents this as a triumph, too. The movie believes that death is the reward for her art, the one way she'll be remembered. Maybe it even believes death is the best thing those like us, who live under otherness's umbra, can get—that only the artists who burn out are to be remembered, that picking up the pieces or moving on isn't a thing of wonder, too.

I can't help but think of the trans women trapped within this same paradigm, the endless lineage of my sisters who struggled in life and soared in death. I can't help but think of the ways we both struggled with our own hard-won desires to live. But while *Black Swan* pools with hate for us like a bee's nest pools with honey, you loved the film and I loved you, so as much as I can intellectualize against it, I must speak of it with love, too. I watched it with you, after all—breathed in your loamy scent next to me, MacBook balanced between our legs, you holding me like I couldn't slip away. Watching it felt like a way to get closer. It wasn't until I rewatched it alone, years later, that I even saw what was wrong with the film, its own cruelty. It wasn't until later that I realized the messiness of the devotion we had.

I've focused on misery for long enough, so when I speak now, I want to speak only of lives happy from the jump, horizons unflecked with fear and selves intact. But to remove fear is to remove pain and to remove pain is to fumigate the cracks in which we live until nothing can live, and I refuse that cruelty, too. I refuse to show our lives less painful but less lived—the opposite of Aronofsky's film, which shows a life filled with pain but absent of anything that indicates Nina is living. I refuse the cruelty of hating the other or the cruelty of wanting to redeem the other through labor or the cruelty of delimiting the other through the shaky dichotomy of the abject. I refuse the obsessive dedication at the expense of selfhood that Aronofsky argues is the closest way to artistic or romantic success, the idea that death is the ultimate cumulation of that dedication. I refuse the notion that alone or not, people can't change, they just fester.

Instead, I redirect that love back onto you and the bruised life we shared. In the background, the sun starts to warm, flecking the tips of my hair with orange. It's 2016, and my eyes are still shut tight, and the morning is starting to break.

Here's what I couldn't say to you that night, what I didn't even know yet. I loved you so much—or I hated myself enough—that I didn't realize I was right in the bathroom stall; I did need to be alone. Only alone can we start to change into the self we need to be, rather than the person we want to be with wants us to be. Like the subtext of any work of horror, my fears of solitude were trying to tell me what I needed all along, but I was too scared to listen. Despite that, I'm glad. Because I didn't, I had my life with you.

In truth, I wasn't asleep when you took the photo. I was fully awake, curling myself into a shape for you. When I saw your text hours later, I responded with surprise, even though the pad of your feet into the room stirred me up right before you snapped the shot. I'll hold that back because I'm scared of sharing everything with you, even though we'll go on to share so much. We'll fumble and fight and try to take space until we do so for good, but the love we have will shape me into who I am today. And so I posed for the photo and allowed myself to become the swan you wanted me to be.

Nina runs her hands along her competitor's stomach and she feels at ease. I turn over on the couch toward you. You click the shutter. Eventually, we will cease to be afraid, and because of that, I will finally leave. But now it's New Year's Day, and we have six and a half years left. Beyond the horizon, the future dances—swanlike, as slow and desperate as we are in the gradually dawning light.

"I was perfect," Nina whispers, and when she dies, it's like she's loved after all.

Our Oceans, Ourselves

1.

There was a drowned girl in our hometown, and we all had to learn her story: an unsolved murder, done by her boyfriend or maybe her father. Her name was Nell Cropsey, and every year, the owners of the house she lived in and died outside of opened it up for a Halloween ghost walk, their pale daughter descending the stairs in a white waterlogged dress. We gathered inside their foyer, a sea of us crammed from the spiral staircase to the elegant lace curtains on the far wall. Nell's name contained *corpse* inside it already; it felt as if she had been destined for her fate.

Nell was a nineteen-year-old who died at the height of the town's prosperity in the early 1900s, which explains part of why she was mythologized in the way she was. Then, unlike now, Elizabeth City was flush with robber barons and cash from the trade routes winding up the Pasquotank River all the way north to the Outer Banks and through the sound to the Chesapeake Bay. Nell's family was rich, too; her house was one of the biggest in town, big enough to have its own name: Seven Pines. The trees swayed in front of and behind the three-story home, and at night, walking past, lights would click on unexpectedly, illuminating the attic or the winding widow's walk along the building's topmost floor.

In eighth grade, we each received a university-press branded biography about her: "The mystery of beautiful Nell Cropsey!" the front cover copy proclaimed above a watercolor etching of her face purpled in the sunset. And she *was* beautiful, especially in the photographs reproduced inside the book. Soft and willowy, her hair curled above her head in a thick brown wave, combed and bobby-pinned in place with precision. Bright tapestries of color whorled across her shoulders. On the cover, the Pasquotank, golden blue and orange, glimmered behind her like a threat. SCHOOL PROPERTY, it said on the back in red-stamped letters, DO NOT STEAL.

In class, we'd debate whether it was her boyfriend or father who killed her, but through the whole set of arguments, I kept seeing her waterlogged, crab-eaten face floating upside-down. It took five months to find her, we learned; five months of dredging the river and looking for her bones. I pictured her underwater that whole time, crowned with river scum and drowned cormorants. But her body had been well-preserved, surprisingly so, for the time she spent submerged; and they found her in a part of the river that had been dredged four times already. She bobbed to the surface clean and pale, no bloating, almost no skin missing, and no water in her lungs, although the autopsy revealed she had been dead since people started searching. Nell Cropsey, the autopsy suggested, hadn't drowned after all. There were other insinuations: As they dredged the river at first, her father's ice bill rose four times higher than usual, as if he was keeping something cold that he valued deeply. But even despite this, everyone in the town still thought of Nell as a drowned girl, the Pasquotank sticking to her sure as glue.

Women pop up dead in water a lot—at least in media they do. Picture the torn, drunk, beach-partying teenager whose death opens *Jaws*, or the opening scene of *Twin Peaks* with Laura Palmer's waterlogged corpse, blue with chill, pulled out of a nearby waterfall. Water's a hazard in these films and TV shows, but never an expected one; women seem to topple suddenly into it and then something underneath gets them. The death itself always comes as a surprise.

Despite what I saw and how I grew up, I never feared water. We lived in a swamp, a thirty-minute drive from a rocky beach known as the Graveyard of the Atlantic. Hurricanes came through yearly, and Elizabeth City would flood every time, muddy water crashing down Main and burying the smaller streets three feet deep along the way. Even in non-hurricane season, the town was dangerous; most everyone knew someone who'd been dragged out by the riptides or got sucked into a muckhole wading the river or flipped their boat near the alligator nest outside the town limits. Every Fourth of July, at least two townies would strip off their clothes, jump into the river, and have to be dragged out minutes later. Water, we were taught, did not take mischief lightly. It sucked you down and held.

I was comforted by the sight of it, though, just as I was later comforted by movies set in the water, too. The expansiveness of the substance calmed me, the surety of something far vaster than my body or the cramped swamp town we lived in. Or maybe it was my childhood memories of swimming in the shimmering Atlantic. Maybe it was even just astrology; I had the most aqueous chart of anyone I knew, as a partner confirmed during a natal reading years later, their eyes widening as they scrolled down their phone.

"*How* many placements in Pisces do you have?" they asked.

"Five," I said, and they let out a long low whistle, and then a guffaw.

"How's it feel to be so crazy?" they asked, and not knowing what else to do, I laughed.

Pisces, the double fish, is the oldest sign in the Zodiac, but paradoxically it's associated with displays of emotion we consider immature: namely, crying. I didn't let anyone see it, but I cried with abundance throughout my life. I cried on late walks by the riverfront, cried listening to lonesome country songs on my battered iPod, cried watching *The Ring* and *The Sixth Sense* and any film involving a child ghost because I identified even then with those deemed unlovable, feared and wondered how quickly I myself could turn. I cried tears of happiness when I was accepted to the residential school in the middle of the state that I thought would be my salvation and tears of sadness when a boy I loved called me a faggot and turned away and tears of every emotion in between. Throughout all of it the water flowed from within to without, an unquenchable reservoir. My sun was in Pisces and my rising was in Pisces and my Mercury, Venus, and Saturn were in Pisces, too, a whole house wriggling like a fish.

Because of all of this, perhaps, I learned the wrong lesson from Nell. Whether or not her body got dumped months later or was just unmolested by the fish and crabs, the fact she was found whole seemed an indication of greater benedictions awaiting. I saw her story fundamentally as a hopeful one, at least in one thin way: You may die, but the water will keep you.

I wanted to be kept so badly. I spent eighth grade almost completely alone, avoiding my home at night and rushing through school during the day. A sadness floated inside me, deep and gnawing, and I thought there was no way to get it out. I was inspired by how Nell was preserved, both in the water and afterward. In the town's collective memory, she stayed young and loved and held forever.

And I wanted to stay held forever. The river was a home, too, I thought, just a dangerous one. Maybe, in the wake of all that sadness, it could be mine as well.

2.

So many ghost stories involve drowning. These ghosts are sad and wet but also tactile, which makes sense. There's a sensuality to water, how it completely fills a space it's put into, only revealing its color in the expanse of a sea or riverbed. There's a sensuality to ghosts, too, floating around like water does, promising a way of moving with less resistance than trudging dirt.

When I felt especially lonely in Elizabeth City, I'd sneak out past 1 or 2 a.m., wandering the streets alone until I ran into someone, which I rarely did. I'd walk past the small spurt of a downtown, the abandoned old library building and the slightly nicer new library building, following the sweet-tea highway of the river and the run-down sidewalks next to it.

Eventually, I'd find myself at the town's water tower. It was past the library, a fat tall iron giant bolted into concrete and protected by one chain-link fence. There wasn't barbed wire on top. You didn't even have to climb the fence; its gate had busted open years ago, so it was easy to push it, barely dangling off one hinge, to the side far enough to squeeze through. Then, you just scurried up the bolted-on ladder until you were on the platform around the tower itself.

I'd sit on the hard iron, iPod earbuds in, feet dangling fifty feet off the ground, and I'd look past the harbor, stare into the faint trickle of boat lights and the highway neon in the distance. I'd stay for thirty, forty-five minutes—sometimes up to an hour—and I'd think of the boy I loved, who had recently betrayed me, and I'd think of Nell's loves, too. Then, waving goodbye to the current lapping against the docks, I'd head back home—only three blocks away from Nell's house, the reflections from the river flickering across the lawn like something still alive.

In *Dark Water*, directed by Hideo Nakata, water is the sign of a haunting but the sign of a home as well. In the 2002 movie, the main character's apartment leaks—water dripping from the walls, the ceiling, the faucets. The leaking is caused by a girl who can command water because that's what killed her, although we don't find that out until the end of the film. In her loneliness she causes harm but is still a hurt person hurting.

Eve Tuck and her collaborator C. Ree write about *Dark Water* in their essay "A Glossary of Haunting." More precisely, they write about justice. Tuck and Ree note that:

> The difference between notions of justice popularized in US horror films and notions of justice in these examples of horror films from Japan is that in the former, the hauntings are positioned as undeserved. . . . In the latter, because the depth of injustice that begat the monster or ghost is acknowledged, the hero does not think herself to be innocent, or try to achieve reconciliation or healing, only mercy.

The early 2000s in America were filled with wearying, Orientalist remakes of mostly Japanese and Korean horror films. J-Horror, they called it, regardless of where the country of origin was. It started, debatably, with Hideo Nakata's earlier, more commercially successful film *Ringu* and its American remake, *The Ring*. In *Ringu*, the characters are complicated. Throughout the film, as the protagonists are guided by ghosts and psychic visions to unearth the past, they discover men exploiting one another and especially exploiting Sadako, a psychic teenager who was used to make her mother—a fraudulent psychic—famous. When the media outs Sadako's mother as a fraud, Sadako kills the journalist who broke the story. Then, her mother is driven to suicide, and eventually Sadako is killed herself, by her father: cycles, or as the movie frames it, rings.

The cycles in *The Ring*, however, are simpler. The most nuanced figure in the film—the mother who kills her own daughter—is smoothed over by the explanation at the end of the movie that Samara Morgan is evil, deserving of the watery end she got. Underneath the text, *The Ring* paints a world where a whole society is guilty of Samara's death, although even the filmmakers don't seem to realize this. Instead, they show a bad child being punished, and a town celebrating.

In *Ringu*, the radius of guilt is narrower, but the rage Sadako feels, if not her humanity, is affirmed. This is even mirrored in the movies' relationships to water: In *Ringu*, we focus on the ocean—immense, uncontainable, a force of nature. But in the American remake, everything circles back to the well, damp and dripping and limited to the place where Samara died—a place, the movie argues, where she belongs.

Tuck and Ree again: "The leak to me is a sort of sign, the ghost's memento mori, that we are always in a process of ruin, a state of ruining." *Dark Water*, which itself was remade into a much narrower, more sentimental American movie three years after it came out, is a far leakier film than *Ringu* or *The Ring*. In Nakata's *Dark Water*, the apartment building is dilapidated, the leaking water as much a measure of the main characters' financial class as of ghosts. Yoshimi, the single mother protagonist, lives in a leaky apartment because she can only afford to live in a leaky apartment. But ghosts of course are tied to and beget from class, too: The mansions of a haunted house and the bereft deprivation of an unmarked grave both point to a disturbance caused by money and its absence as much as by other violences.

The wide range of meanings that wetness takes on in these movies make sense; water is never just one thing. Access to it unfettered is a matter of racial, economic, and colonial justice—as the histories of pipeline resistance, Flint, Palestine, and countless other places insist. But water is also ruin, flooding and seeping with regularity, and those who face the aftereffects of that water most immediately are bound by their class, too. After all, the signs of a flood are most visible to those who cannot afford to move out of water's reach: a yellowed wall, a wrecked engine, a cavernous concrete block of apartments dripping. It's not coincidental that these images—a wet ceiling, a rusted and poorly cleaned water tank—are the central ones of *Dark Water*. Maybe this is what Tuck and Ree mean by a state of ruining: Look at this world. Ghosts are everywhere.

So the question drowned ghosts ask is a direct one: What do we owe those who have been wronged? This is the fulcrum on which *Dark Water* turns, the question my college partner, a butch with choppy orange hair and pilgrim steppers, asked me after we finished watching it the first time. We watched in a big group late at night, all of us huddled on my dorm room bed; we hadn't even started dating yet, but our hands brushed underneath my sheets. The group talked through the whole film, but by the end, everyone fell silent: Yoshimi sacrificing herself to mother the drowned child ghost, saving her own child's life in the process. Yoshimi, the film seems to say, owes the dead her physical body. Water, which doesn't have a conscience, or at least doesn't have a conscience easy for humans to understand, would suggest we owe our presence. A memento mori remembers that you die, but beyond that, it just remembers.

The butch and I went on to date for about a year: We'd watch scary movies together, the first partner who I really started to do that with. We'd get into fights. And we'd talk about where we were born: them, a scrappy trailer in the boonies of Appalachia, and me, the Virgin Islands. I'd tell them about what stuck with me from Saint Thomas, which I could barely remember.

In the first photo of me I know of, I'm floating on my back, sea around me. It's so bright cerulean it almost looks like I'm in a swimming pool—but I'm not, my mother swears. "That's the ocean!" she says, and in the photo my smile is so large and at ease it almost pierces through the frame. I'm young, barely several months old, held afloat by a plastic set of water wings. Beyond the frame, my father's hands are almost invisible, fading as the photo has with age and, as the picture was kept in our bathroom, water stains, too.

In Saint Thomas, we weren't tourists, but we were interlopers from the mainland. The shining beaches, deep blue water, were all ours because we said they were. And when we left the island, when I was four, it was naturalized to the point of not even feeling like an option, parents hopping from job to job until they both found security in the tangle of the swamp fifty minutes from the coast of North Carolina, where we settled and where I grew up.

The politics of being white interlopers on a majority Black island were lost on me as an infant. But they became increasingly less so as I got older and read Caribbean writers more critical of my family's position—which was, in its spectacular departures and arrivals, actually more touristic than not. "Every native everywhere lives a life of overwhelming and crushing banality and desperation and depression," Jamaica Kincaid writes about her own small island of Antigua. "Every native would like a tour. But some natives—most natives in the world—cannot go anywhere. . . . They are too poor to escape the reality of their lives." Perhaps my mother and father went to Saint Thomas because they wanted to escape their own realities, but in doing so, supplanted another. They both were poor, young—"in search," as my mother would say, "of adventure." Then, a terrible thing happened: My sister, their daughter, died. She was nineteen—the same age as Nell Cropsey when she passed—and two years later I was born. Drowning in grief with a newborn baby, the adventure ended, and my parents moved back to the mainland. But they were able to escape both times—first, to the island; and then, away.

I said that water doesn't have a conscience, but maybe it's more accurate to say that a conscience, like most of water, is only visible under certain conditions. We just don't have the means to view it. Almost every body of water that whirls with silt or mud becomes difficult to see in past five or six feet at a time. But, in a plastic bucket or palmed in a hand, almost all water is crystalline.

I heard that when we lived in Saint Thomas, this was one of my favorite things to do. I'd laugh with delight as I scooped out fistfuls of ocean, especially around sunset; deep and expansive, the purpled and orangey water would turn clear in my palms. Then, I'd open them to return it back to the sea it came from and immediately the color changed to something darker, the water harder to look through again. I could only understand water when I confined it, filtered it out palm after palm. But that unseeable part, unknowable and deep, is perhaps where the water's conscience actually lies.

In our family bathroom in Elizabeth City, I'd wash my hands and stare at the picture of baby me, wondering what I was thinking. I look glowing, happy, like there's nowhere beyond the ocean I'd rather be. But the water obscures this picture, too: I can't see past my wings. Even my feet are distorted by ripples and brownish water damage creasing the page.

The image that sticks with me the most from our first viewing of *Dark Water* is of the girl, filmed from below, floating in the water tank before she died. Did she dream while she was floating? Did she feel joy, or loss, or sorrow? Did she rage against those who built the building she died in in the first place? Maybe grief, like justice, isn't confined to just one feeling. Maybe it billows outward, like water or blood. The thing is, if a container of water is large enough, it looks like there's no container at all.

3.

Several years ago, I attended a writing residency at a water research center. Previously a hunting lodge in Pennsylvania, the grounds were on a lake untapped and, as such, unpolluted. The landowner wanted the lake for his own private fishing, so refused to let any of the locals in, to fish or even to swim. Because of his avarice, it wound up being one of the cleanest in the state.

Thermometers bobbled off the docks, and we were instructed firmly to stay out of the testing facility, a large, locked shed on the lakefront. Every morning when I woke, I'd clamber into a canoe, splashing myself with the paddle as I passed the scientists collecting samples to test the purity and O_2 levels of the bright surface. There we'd go, me paddling further into the lake and them walking back to the shed with their samples.

There'd be eggs and pancakes once I returned to the house, but usually by the time I arrived they'd be cold. I preferred to spend my mornings in solitude on the lake, and because I was a late riser, this precluded me from seeing my fellow residents. I missed the early morning conversations and the hot food, but otherwise didn't mind. The water felt like its own sort of kinship, the thin gray of mist cutting through the thicker gray of the lake.

There wasn't one lake at the residency, though; there were two. Soon the landowner, I was told, grew bored of the hunting and fishing he had available, so he evacuated a nearby hamlet to make a reservoir. It was at the edge of his property, spanning almost a mile, and at the center of it, a hundred feet down, the town still bubbled underneath. He moved nothing, just flooded the valley instead.

I went swimming in the second lake my first day there, before I even canoed. I forgot to pack my bathing suit, so I skinny-dipped; at first, I was afraid of getting hit by one of the burly men I saw piloting speedboats around the far corner of the lake, and then once I remembered the reality of my body, I was afraid of just being sighted. But no one saw me and the water felt sharp and relieving, running across my belly and down my legs and pricking my nipples slightly up with cold as I surfaced from it. As I shook my hair dry, droplets stained the rocks a darker shade of gray and I almost slipped back into the water. Instead, though, I steadied myself, wriggled my panties and threadbare tank top back on, wrapped myself in the towel I left folded on the rocky shore, and headed back to the house.

I was talking to the groundskeeper over dinner when I found out about the bodies underneath the water. I mentioned to him I had swam in the second lake, as we were warned we could contaminate the delicate pH balance of the first one, ruining weeks of tests. I knew of the town there below, the destruction the landowner wreaked to have access to more water. He raised an eyebrow when I mentioned how refreshing the swim was and cleared his throat.

"Everyone swims there," he said. "But everyone also knows they didn't move the cemetery when they evacuated the town."

When a body is put in water, the water dilutes it, but the body dilutes the water, too: less river, more flesh. Maybe the water was sluiced through with ghosts. Maybe because I passed through it, my body was sluiced through, too. I showered immediately afterward, but it was within me. It couldn't come out.

Did those underwater feel me as I swam one hundred feet above where they were still buried? It had been almost a hundred years, so surely the water and fish and silt whittled them almost completely down. Were they "they" still, or had they become lake?

But even now I prioritize my own perspective, not the water's. Perhaps instead of saying that I passed through them, it would be more accurate to suggest they, still alive, pass through me. Perhaps I myself am not owing the dead in that water what they deserve.

A ghost, maybe, is a thing that can never be dry.

In Elizabeth City, when I—still a child myself—climbed the water tower and looked out over the narrow sprawl of the town, I would sometimes start to weep. I felt full with a sadness I didn't know how to trace yet, so the crying came out in its place. Barely lit by the dim orange streetlights sixty feet down, I'd wipe my nose with the back of my hand, tears pinking my face and curving down my lips. Once, I saw a lone drop wobble off my chin and fall down until it was impossible to see, a clear ball lost in the spiky green grass below.

Nell Cropsey, on the cover of the book we read, also cried. One opal tear rolled down her face as she looked up and toward her right shoulder: A hand rested there, heavy and large, presumably that of her killer.

As an eighth grader, I liked that mirroring, tied together as it was by the menace of the hand on her shoulder. I stared at the cover for hours after the book was assigned to us. Water lurked behind her and on her, although in very different ways, the river and the tear; past and future separated from each other by the peachy skin of the stranger's hand looming toward her death.

Tears are a sign of crisis or bereavement, but most directly, they're a sign of water exiting the body. As a child, every time I cried, I thought it a small marvel. I pictured a reservoir of water inside my head holding all the tears I would ever cry. As I cried, I pictured the tears inside me emptying out a wet hole until it became dry: an abscess, a dried-out riverbed, a well.

Things aren't supposed to be wet, or at least humans aren't; even after a shower, even after my swim in the lake, I reach immediately for a towel. When I cry, though, I almost never wipe my face. This water produced by me, I let stay. Maybe it's my Pisces stellium, but tears have always felt redemptive—revealing the heart of an emotion immediately in a way that can't easily be concealed. Tears communicate the same way that other water does, quiet but pervasive in their strength.

But tears are weapons, too. With the exception of *Dark Water* and a few other films, the canon of the drowned is a canon of whiteness. Leo sinking beneath the water in *Titanic*. A fisherman's son in *I Know What You Did Last Summer*, hit with a car and stuffed in the trunk and dropped in the surf off Wilmington. The TV leaking, Rachel's eyes widening, in the American version of *The Ring*. Surely you've noticed this. The drowned girl is a pale girl, which is to say she's pale already, which is to say she's not made pale but born, further bleached by the current and cold. Our pain, the drowned, is visible because it's a white pain, just like Nell's death was white pain, just like white tears are white pain, and this pain can easily target anything or anyone not white. In fact, it's meant to. It's in the design.

Even the fact that Nell's death was taught to us in the eighth grade fits this plan. According to the 2021 census, white people make up 36 percent of Elizabeth City's population. Yes, our Honors English class was highly segregated and whiter than the rest of the town by a significant margin. But this just underscores the point. A room mainly made up of white students in a school mainly made of up Black ones spent a month on her, intentionally or not learning the ways her innocence was violated to instill the fear of our own being taken away, too. She shaped our lives, just like the ghost walk shaped the way history was remembered in the town. Nell Cropsey became our education. We were kept as sure as she was.

In college, it was up to me to preserve my own body. This was how I discovered that drinking water during sex was the easiest way to avoid slipping away, to find myself again. I drank glass after glass, felt it rolling inside me. Hydrated, my desires were tempered, mutable enough to fit inside a palm or a bucket. I'd never explain what I was doing, but eventually lovers would catch on and it became a shared habit, their own water glasses perched next to mine on the end tables: we'd fuck, stop, take a sip, and resume again. As I drank, I'd rush back into myself sudden as an orgasm, present again to an intoxicating degree. Even now, as I have sex sometimes, I feel a rising presence, the tail of something barely noticeable as I approach climax. Drinking water amplifies it, and in moments of pleasure I feel a wave cresting, a ghost I don't know yet as my whole body shudders beneath a lover's touch. Desire transforms you—but it does so slowly, through accumulation. Gradually, the more I slept with people, the more their wants became my own. Like a riverbed, my body grew to bear the imprint of everyone who's visited it before.

But you can't have desire without pain, and when I first experimented with polyamory my junior year of college, I fucked the butch's friend. They were devastated afterward, and I remembered (how could I forget?) that they had a crush on the same friend. "How could you do this to me?" they asked, and tears streamed down their face. I had no clue. Pisces are supposed to be the sign most receptive to others' emotions, which makes us more receptive to the spirit world as well. However, I had no idea how much my actions, which felt so hopeful at the time, would hurt them.

Immediately after they confronted me, I burst into tears, too, and that seemed like it resolved things: us both crying, the conversation fizzling to a halt. But of course it didn't resolve things, because nothing changed. I kept sleeping around, and the tension in our relationship continued building, running underneath it all as sure as a secret river twines down beneath a city. "It wasn't me," one could say, and I did. "I was compelled to."

And then, for the next several years, sure as the surf, I would mechanically find myself entangled with others, downing cup after cup of bright water all the while. When I think of ghosts, I think of a communion of unknown figures homing themselves in my home, finding themselves in my body—but I also think of the people I hurt by fucking the ones they cared about too. My tears excused me, but also nothing was excused. It just continued. I remembered what had been taught to me. I cried my white tears.

Nell Cropsey never had sex, we learned in eighth grade—although she did purportedly flirt with other men to try to provoke her boyfriend into proposing, which he was incensed by. This was never emphasized in my education, though. Her virginity was what made her so innocent, and her death so tragic. It contextualized the whole story, even adding its aura to the cover of the book we read: on her shoulder, the hand of a murderer but also maybe a lover. The water behind her beckoning with invitation, almost a baptism, changing the context surrounding her body and what would be done with it but never reaching its conclusion. And Nell, skin almost translucent in the setting sun, wealth hoarded behind her, inviting one's sympathy all the while.

When I returned to look at the cover of *The Mystery of Beautiful Nell Cropsey* while writing this essay, though, I found that I had fabricated Nell's tears. Her eyes were wide with fear, true, but unwelled, her face dry. I imagined the wetness gleaming there, which means the tears weren't hers, or even the book cover's artist's. They were my own. Sure, crying yields an escape from responsibility for some bodies, some people. But how much did I myself hunger for that escape? How much did I already practice it, alone or together? A lover, after all, can both hold and betray, as the river did, too. A tear can both illuminate and distract, can tell its own lies or mistruths.

"I've only been to the ocean twice," the butch had said early in our relationship. "I don't even know how it would feel to grow up surrounded by it. It seems beautiful."

We can tell a story about Nell crying, but who cries over her? And who else is left in the water, unmourned?

4.

Most of the pain involved in drowning comes from breathing in water. In a literature review conducted in 2020 of near-death experiences while drowning, there was a dramatic difference between those who aspirated and those who did not. Those for whom water entered the lungs described intense pain, an "awful struggle" that went on for minutes. But those who didn't breathe all the way in felt comparative comfort the whole way through. In *Dark Water*, we don't see the child aspirating; that would perhaps be too cruel. Nell, too, was unconscious, they say, when she entered the water (the autopsy revealed a blow to her temple), and because of that, her lungs were freed from pain.

Most drownings happen at night—at least that was what my

mother told me. I was lonely as a child, and what I liked about water was that it seemed lonely, too. Whenever we stayed overnight at the beach, I'd walk out to the surf, watch the waves go in and out sparkling beneath the star-struck sky. "I don't want two dead children," she said once when she caught me wading into the surf after dinner. But once I got older, I would slip out regularly and go swimming at night anyway, darting under the waves lit only by the full pale moon. I didn't worry about death at all, staying out until my fingers pruned. Instead, swimming at night felt like a practice of kinship: I was the water and the water was me. She called, and I half-listened so many times.

The tensest moment in *Dark Water* is when Yoshimi, beleaguered, climbs the water tank. She knows what's inside but is terrified to find out. In fact, the instant we see the water tank, we know. We see the elevator that goes up to the roof; we see the ghost child disappearing again and again throughout the film. Every other hiding place, at this point, has been exhausted. For once, we see what carries the water, but not the water itself. And then, in flashback, we see the child climbing up the side of the tank and floating. Watching the movie under our blanket, the butch's hands tightened against mine. We both drew a breath.

Drowning is terrifying for the living, but for the dying it seems to feel like coming home. In the studies quoted, participants talked about their bodies flooding with numbness, joy, calm. Some saw lights. One participant reported a barrage of rendingly gorgeous colors: "Seashells," she described, "sea fish, quiet, beautiful, as my body slowly drifted down, down, down." According to her, it was the most pleasant experience of her life. But she didn't aspirate; when they found her, her lungs were free of water.

"If you die drowning, I would say it's one of the more peaceful ways to go," said another, who did breathe in. "After the worst fifteen minutes of your life, that is."

To die by drowning, then, is to not feel alone.
I don't know what Nell or the child felt.

The residency with the two lakes, and what the landowner did to form that second lake, wasn't unique. Countless towns were flooded to form bodies of water. Most of them were homes to poor people or Black people or Indigenous people or all three, a reflection of the larger violence this country has waged since its founding. It's hard to estimate how many times this has happened, given the tendency of the oppressor to hide what he does to the oppressed—but it's safe to assume every artificial lake or reservoir constructed with government Works Project money during the great boom of the 1930s came about this way, to say nothing about what shaped the private and public bodies of water before and after, whose histories were left off a public ledger. There could be hundreds of them. There could be thousands.

The most famous of these, Lake Lanier in Georgia, used to be an autonomous Black community named Oscarville. In 1912, a white woman was raped and murdered near there, dumped in the Chattahoochee River. White townsfolk nearby pinned her death on four young Black men, and the white people formed a lynch mob, forced everyone from their houses and land in Oscarville, and murdered the four men, widely believed to be innocent. They pillaged the land, and out of the force of this violence Oscarville was abandoned shortly thereafter; what remained was ransacked over until nothing was left. By the 1950s, the US Army arrived to force the area's scant remaining inhabitants off the land, and the valley Oscarville was a part of got filled in to make Lake Lanier. The lake is now currently a vacation home destination for America's white upper crust again.

The lake has a reputation for being haunted, albeit one not ungrounded; over five hundred people have died there since the lake's construction. There are countless ghost stories that proliferate about Lanier's shore—the few residents forced to leave in the '50s coming back for revenge, the first drowning victims found in Lanier's depths contributing to every other death. But if we're entertaining these ghost stories, the violence the lake was founded on is the most obvious cause of any haunting: a white woman whose death was used to kill four Black men and destroy countless more lives afterward. As the area is now majority white, those who drown now are white, too. As far as I know, their deaths have not been used to cause any more death in turn.

Nell's boyfriend, Jim Wilcox, was blamed most for her murder. He was white and working class and had a temper, with most of the trial documents emphasizing his "breeding" and manners—an 1800s Republican family, a history of manual labor at the shipyard, a proclivity for practical jokes and sudden rages. Wilcox was almost hanged by a mob the day he was arrested under suspicion for her murder; they stormed the courthouse. It was only his whiteness that saved him, the prison guard's willingness to turn the mob away.

That was why the conspiracy theory that her father killed Nell appealed to me so much: the idea that, even as murders were so often carried out by someone close to you, there was always someone closer who could evade suspicion. That wealth and privilege and centrality to power insulates you from blame. It's not that the death of white women is always used to punish those excluded, by choice or by circumstance, from a community. But in every wet-gulletted throat there lurks a potential means to an already-anticipated end, and maybe Nell's father saw his chance as sure as every other rich murderer does.

What surprised me the most about *Dark Water* is that there was no one to blame for the ghost girl's death at all. When we see her die in flashback, I braced myself for another twist. Where was the figure luring her to the roof with candy and a devious purpose in mind? Surely someone was responsible for the flood she unleashed onto the apartments below her. Did her mother snap and force her to die? But there was no villain: Even the girl, the antagonist of the film, is just a scared child. The blame, such that it existed, lay with lax safety measures in place, a mother who vanishes from their home and a daughter who roams free in her absence, a once-yearly water tank cleaning schedule that the child unwittingly takes advantage of. We're unused to a death that exists without motive, and when I finished the film, the ending almost felt unsatisfying. Now though, it feels like a promise, another way to think about this all. Guilt, and responsibility, are both diffuse. To blame one person is to miss the point of how these systems work.

This is evident, again, in the difference between the American and Japanese *Dark Waters*; in the remake, there's a cover-up, an explicitly abusive mother, a paid-off building manager—everything the Japanese film was wise enough to avoid. The American film takes on the logic of the procedural; in the Japanese film, the child's death is just a terrible thing that happens, and it flows out like water. The scariest thing for Americans, the change implies, is death without explanation—and for the American movie, made at least in part to cash in on a trend, there's nothing commercially promising about a badness that lingers.

I'm indebted to the same rotted thinking, though. My own earlier focus on who killed Nell also distracted from these realities of her life, attempted to map a sense of justice and responsibility onto a senseless death. I realize now that Nell Cropsey was killed because, often, people kill women, and if they are white, that death is mythologized afterward. Which isn't to say my dead girl shouldn't be remembered by the town, although I have suspicions of that remembrance now. It's just that the things revealed by her death are not what the narrative I was taught suggests they should be.

It doesn't matter if Nell Cropsey died in the river or not. What matters is that was where she was found, and where her ghost, if it exists, lives to this day. What matters is that her story was linked to the water, molded by it as the town was as well. It wasn't that she was our history; it was that the river was, and everything the river preserved.

What I wish I had realized, sitting on the tower or wading out in the river, was that water shaped everything in the town. It had its own desires, and they mixed with mine, too, sure as a lover's do. During hurricane season in Elizabeth City, waves would crash down the street, rain pouring sideways and gutters spitting out their contents. When the sewers got too full, the contents mingled in the street, and you'd see children playing, splashing up and down like they would with a busted fire hydrant. Everywhere was shaped by the tide.

The town used to be a swamp; when it was stolen from those who lived here before and live here still and when the swampy shores of the river were paved over to make a city—a city that in its own mythology predated the United States even though it wasn't formally founded until 1801, that was seized during the Civil War and used as a military encampment by the Union, that attempted to massacre the Tuscarora people and failed before that, that committed countless other murders less remembered, that grew richer and richer with shipping money until its waterways fell into disuse after the turn of the century, around Nell's death, the one death that was remembered, a death that shaped our education inside and outside of school—we, the inhabitants, lost our capacity to hold anything. But water doesn't need to hold; it can drip, and fill, and betray, and love almost anything. That was what made the ghost in *Dark Water* so scary to me, why Nell Cropsey's death filled me with such obsession: Like the sea, it was unquenchable. As a young child, I felt joy there, but even that joy was wide and unquenchable, too. Yes, growing up we left the island for North Carolina, but the water came with us. Now every year, sure as clockwork, it courses out like it always does and makes the formerly wet land we called ours wet again.

When I climbed up the water tower as a teenager, I didn't realize I was by enough water to kill me. I wouldn't realize that, in fact, until years later, when I watched *Dark Water* for the first time. Instead, sitting on the tower, I just knew the water was inside, and I was outside, and I was dry. I'd stare at the harbor, and before that, the swamp; I would smell the tannins in the air. I'd think of being loved, not the ways I'd betray those who'd love me. I'd think about breathing in.

Ghost Face

1.

There's no ruin, no urban decay in the original *Scream*. It's all clean white interiors, a gently pastoral landscape for the Hollywood-professional class to relax in splendor. Girls lived in sprawling forested suburban homes, all large wraparound porches and open floor plans and stairways with generous banisters. There was something resplendent about it, an open-palmed white Northern California wealth completely unfamiliar to me. Houses like that just didn't exist in Elizabeth City—or if they did, I didn't know their inhabitants.

Instead, my town sat squatter, flatter, and more cramped than the space I saw on screen. Our streets were less well-maintained; our geographies less clearly delineated. The closest thing we had to the movie's neighborhoods were the multistory white Victorians spread out in rows by the river, standing in formation with oak and sumac trees. A girl I had a crush on in early high school lived in one of those places; I only sometimes visited her home, but we'd talk on the phone for hours most evenings, handheld cradled under my ear, door locked tightly. There, I'd imagine her pacing in her sprawling home as I paced in mine, and I'd rewatch movies like *Scream* that told me that her sort of life—spacious, be-tree-d, spotless, yet still vulnerable to harm—was the average. We kissed once in the dilapidated fitness center that Hurricane Isabel destroyed in 2003 and told each other ghost stories afterward, before the short bike ride back home. Then she went back to her boyfriend, queer dalliance over.

Elizabeth City, North Carolina, is quiet, hermetic, majority Black, mainly poor, and deeply segregated. As part of a mostly failed tourism strategy, there are faded murals everywhere up and down the Pasquotank River proclaiming it the "Harbor of Hospitality"—free boat parking for forty-eight hours, soused white yachters stumbling down the boardwalk to the one seafood restaurant in town. It has an HBCU and the largest Coast Guard base—the whitest branch of the U.S. military, according to a 2021 internal survey—on the East Coast. Even the two town cemeteries are segregated.

Growing up, I could bike everywhere. I biked to the Blockbuster. I biked to the Food Lion with spare change to get dinner. I biked to friends' houses, leaving in the morning on breezy summer days and not heading home until late evening. Hurricane after hurricane had knocked most of the trees in town down and what survived was knobbled with cypress knees, thin twigs of branches; I biked past those, too. There was a yearly Halloween spirit walk in the old houses lining the waterfront, the inhabitants of the richer part of town slipping on moldering white dresses and pretending to be their dead ancestors. Fliers would litter my bike routes, and so I went every year.

I hated the South and living there. Biking past the remnants of downtown, I set my sights on better coasts and fixed myself on who I could have been if born elsewhere.

My first job, at ten, was as a junior docent for the local museum. I received an oversize polo, free admission during weekdays, a tiny stipend, and a hefty pack of lies to recite about the accomplishments of our town. On museum tours, we'd walk past murals of cooperation between the Pasquotank people whose land the museum was named after and the white colonizers whose descendants operated the space, the murals of the Confederate soldiers buried in the graveyard behind the museum marching in formation, the etching of the town engulfed in Union forces during the Civil War. We learned to tell a story where we were the heroes. Sometimes, we talked about pirates.

I wasn't an exceptional student, but in the museum, standing in the shadowy timbers of a restored frontier home, I learned the stories asked of me. There's a photo of me in front of that building's gabled eaves, long blond hair blowing in the breeze, an early growth spurt sending me shooting up above the rest of the junior docents. Amid the weight of this history, I looked at ease.

The thing about growing up in the rural South is that it's so easy to fantasize about living anywhere else. In the 2000s landscape I came of age in, California was *the* fantasy. Red Hot Chili Peppers constantly played on the alternative radio station beaming in from the Outer Banks; half the shows marketed toward me, from *The O.C.* to most of the CW's programming block, centered the unexpected adventures and easy living on the West Coast. Even the tomboyish clothing I wore—skinny jeans and hoodies, Billabong and Volcom and Vans that I got from the skate shop during yearly sales—carried the weight of their original state inside every tiny pocket. White culture at the time *was* California culture.

But it wasn't the radio, or television, or even clothes that caused me to fantasize about California; it was *Scream*. Everything else in popular culture I saw carried a masculine prankish sheen overpowering the parts that seemed otherwise compelling, all rowdy shirtless men in bands and softboy bravado. In *Scream,* the snark was feminized. Sidney Prescott, the film's protagonist, told the white-faced, hooded killer to fuck off as easily as she did the men. And because of that, perhaps, I seized onto the movie, projecting a place that wasn't here onto it: a sunny, woodsy escape from the South toward something else completely different. I disliked the tone at first—too jokey, too casual, smug in an almost cash-grabby way—but something in the movies, even watching them a half decade after their release, kept drawing me back.

The basic plot of *Scream* is as follows: A young, rich white girl is brutally stabbed to death in her home alone, watching a scary movie. Within several days, a police investigation and media circus both descend on her high school, doofy but well-meaning cops trying to stop further murders. But it's to no avail: The principal is killed, then another girl. A party is thrown at a large country house and the police infiltrate it. Eventually, we find out the killer is the main character's preppy boyfriend. The boyfriend's best friend, who is clearly in love with him, helps with the murders, staining his loose-fitting sweater crimson with blood. As the two friends stab each other, making it seem like they're victims in the killings, too, it almost looks like they're making love.

Growing up, I'd escape my neighborhood to gather in my friends' spacious foyers, settling into long leather couches to watch rich people play video games. I envied everything about them. My own family—parents who taught at the local college and lived in a vinyl-sided house several blocks up from the waterfront—wasn't poor, but we didn't seem to have everything like my wealthier friends did: no leather couches, no banistered stairs, no multiple sets of video game consoles. We stayed in Elizabeth City because that was where their jobs were, but also because, in my father's words, money stretched further there. By our third year, we had settled; to live in another city, another state—my parents seemed to think—was unimaginable. I didn't even know what the suburbs were. I thought *Scream* was set in a small woodsy town like our own, but one filled with the wealthy instead of our working-class neighbors.

But *Scream*'s metaphor of a town's big hidden secret catalyzing the violence it faces still made sense to me. The movie, after all, is about the legacy of unprocessed trauma. Sidney's mother was murdered a year before the events of *Scream*, and everyone urges her to get over it already—and the fact that she doesn't fuels the resentment Sidney's boyfriend Billy feels toward her and the rest of the town. ("When are you going to let [your mom's death] go, Sid?" he asks her when she won't fuck him, "You have to move on.") All of this takes place against the backdrop of an increasing media frenzy as reporter

Gale Weathers—who wrote a previous exposé on Sidney's mother's own murder—descends on the scene of the crimes. She's a successful reporter, the movie argues, because she's emboldened by the knowledge that salacious violence is her ticket to the top. Throughout the film, death is omnipresent yet regarded with snark, sarcasm, and a teenage eye-roll—an exhausting inconvenience or meal ticket to everyone but Sidney herself.

I didn't see my reflection in *Scream*; I saw aspiration. On the phone with my friend with the wraparound porch, I'd fantasize about escapes—first to the more progressive middle of the state and then to another place entirely. Yes, the characters in *Scream* were all fuckups, but they were rich fuckups, California fuckups, and I hungered for them. In the movie, I could see a potential future free of the South: the big houses and long lawns and raucous parties in the film a beacon, less a sign of violence than one of promise. The murders in the film aren't reckonings; they're thrills. From where I stood, something was wrong in Elizabeth City in a less thrilling way, and I learned to feel ashamed of anyone who stayed there, regardless of family or community obligations or economics keeping them. So when I saw my opportunity to leave, I jumped—just like my parents had for their own thrills in the Caribbean years earlier.

Actual economic deprivation doesn't seem to exist in *Scream*. There, only one of the teens worked. Doing shifts at the video store, Randy Meeks shocks customers, slacks on the job, and gets fired repeatedly. We never see where he lives, but everyone else in the film resides in the same big homes as the straight girl I'd talk to. Poor people aren't in the first *Scream*. "I thought Blockbuster fired you," a character asks Randy, and he clarifies "Twice," but this is meant to show his devotion to movies, not his desperation for employment.

Economic desperation didn't exist in the worlds of my upper-crust friends, either. Everyone jaunted between school and their ample homes, money not an issue at all. There, no one worked because no one had to. People like the girl I had a crush on owned Elizabeth City, and they turned it into what it was: a rickety mass of depreciating real estate, pooling power within its swampy borders. *Big and lonely* is how *Scream*'s script describes all the houses. Or, once, *big and ominous*. Sure as a knife sliding into a breast, every one of my friends—their preplanned careers, their dazzling white houses and teeth and skin, their entire lives out ahead of them—could just be.

2.

On April 21, 2021, a Black Lives Matter movement activated in Elizabeth City in response to the police killing of Andrew Brown Jr., a 42-year-old man executed outside his own home. Because of the size of the town, he lived less than a mile away from me. He lived, in fact, right behind the museum.

Over the next several weeks, from my one-bedroom apartment in Brooklyn, I watched videos of the protests on YouTube and checked updates on the social media accounts of the people I knew who still lived in the area. I set up Google News alerts and pressed refresh on the Democracy Now! homepage, which had started to cover the protests sparingly. I donated to bail funds and shared calls for supplies and mutual aid in Elizabeth City among my larger networks. Through the smudged glass of the laptop, I saw videos of protestors walking down the same empty thoroughfares I used to: past the Food Lion, the now-abandoned Blockbuster, the harbor. The girl I had kissed outside the fitness center, who still lived in the state, posted a lone fist emoji on Facebook. Before, I had to explain to friends where Elizabeth City was; now, dizzyingly, other people were talking about the place like they knew it.

Because of my own immune issues, I didn't show up in person for the great wave of protests in 2020, instead staying home listening to police scanners, texting friends on the ground, doing bail support from my bed. And although I had been vaccinated and finally started to feel comfortable taking part in actions again, I felt by going back down to Elizabeth City I'd be asserting a narrative of my own belonging that wasn't true. By high school, my friend group had almost completely segregated, a flood of mainly white faces stretching wide as the banks of our river, white as the cast of *Scream* itself. To show up in my former town now, I felt, would rewrite my past history and make myself into a hero, another white girl who always knew the stakes. My family didn't even live there anymore, moving away as I was midway through college. Even as I nightly regretted my decision not to carpool down, I didn't want to be a tourist.

But tourism was what I had learned. Growing up, none of the docents for the museum were Black, nor any of the full-time staff. It wasn't till I left the state that I learned of the progressive history of my hometown, one hidden from everyone within its borders: some 50,000 Black Maroons escaping enslavement to form a collectively run commune in the depths of the swamp, walking the same land we did on their way there—shadows of the cabins they built, shards of pots and tools still being excavated today. None of this history was described or declaimed by the museum—just as the so-called Tuscarora War one county over, the largest-scale act of Indigenous resistance in North Carolina proper, wasn't described either. Apart from the stolen names for our streets and waterways—Tuscarora Avenue, Perquimans Avenue, the Pasquotank River—anything outside the rigid proprieties of the colony was erased completely. Instead, the museum sat, escapist.

By the middle of high school, I had planned my getaway: first to a school in the middle of the state, then a college farther away in the mountains, then finally New York after graduation, crashing on my older sister's pullout until I found my own place. I celebrated my own plans for departure, saw it as a rejection of the quiet desperation of the swamp. I thought in leaving I was separating the segregation and meanness I learned in Elizabeth City from myself, but I was wrong. I could never do that.

Forget *Scream*. What I remembered watching the protests around Andrew Brown Jr.'s death was that not everyone else in Elizabeth City could or even wanted to get out. Their homes were here, hard-won in the face of the segregation and ever-present policing of the town. The cracking-apart streets, the knobby cypress knees pointing straight up out of the water, the chants of the crowd as they marched up Water Street. There is no metaphor here: A man died. This was someone's life.

In 2019, my partner Avery and I finally visited California, ten years after I left Elizabeth City forever and five years after we both left the South. We went to Los Angeles, to see one friend who moved to Oakland right after we booked our plane tickets and another who was too ill for company the whole time we were there. So it was just us by ourselves. It was early November, the temperature balmy and Christmas decorations everywhere.

We wanted to go there to escape the clawing cold of New York late fall, but also, I suspect, because my own childhood longing for the state still dwelled within me. As we walked along narrow steep sidewalks, though (too narrow for a wheelchair, our friend messaged us with frustration), we saw the same violence we were used to, just gauzier in the West Coast sun: the same displacement of houseless people, the same fitness ladies bouncing up and down in Lululemon and drinking $15 kale smoothies, the same air of barely concealed white superiority. It was just California-ized, marketed with more faux-concern for the health of the visitors there. During our stay, our Airbnb host would squint her eyes, point at me and say: "This one? Very pretty. But you"—pointing at my partner—"are too fat." Unlike Avery, I had passed as normative, and I was safe.

These things were all in *Scream* as well, but they were mainly there through their absence: As my friend Lea reminded me on the phone, there is not a single non-white person in the entire first movie. (The sequels attempted to course-correct, albeit in queasy ways. *Scream 2* opens with a Black woman, played by Jada Pinkett Smith, criticizing the tacit racism of horror as a genre; she's stabbed in front of a cheering live audience in the most brutal death in the film. *Scream 5* and *Scream 6*, soft-reboots of the franchise, feature two Latina sisters, played by Melissa Barrera and Jenna Ortega, as the main protagonists; during the production of *Scream 7*, Barrera was fired for her pro-Palestinian social media posts and Ortega resigned due to scheduling issues, at least according to the production company.) There is nothing unique in how this one horror movie projected its shallow hierarchies of selfhood onto the state: The erasures of Black people, Indigenous people, Latinx and Asian people all living in California, the way only rich neighborhoods were depicted, these things are in almost every movie. But because *Scream* was what I latched onto as I daydreamed escape, the resonance was a more immediate and deeply felt one. Our museum, after all, erased the lives of people of color in the town, too; our museum made us the hero as well.

Maybe the screenwriter of *Scream* felt the same way, too. Kevin Williamson grew up in semirural North Carolina himself, living in New Bern with his fisherman parents. Williamson was gay, although he didn't start dating until he was in his late twenties. After college, like me, he moved immediately to New York. And then he wound up in Los Angeles and started making his career, where he wrote the movie that made him famous.

"*Scream*," Williamson said in an interview, "is about gay survival." The things I warmed to in the first film—the quips, the complex women, the homoeroticism of the ending—are all shared across a lot of queer media. But if you look beyond the universal queerness the film promises, it's not about gay survival after all: It's about gay escape. Other things Williamson did—*I Know What You Did Last Summer, Dawson's Creek*—are awash in the specifics of North Carolina. But *Scream* has none of that. Everyone in the movie is confident in California, because they were born there. It's a world where race doesn't exist, where class doesn't exist: a fiction far from the South. *Scream* is set in a world, somewhere, where the only thing you have to deal with is trauma.

Avery and I only saw some of the wealth in LA: blithe hipsters in Echo Park, a set of acquaintances who lived in a Fallingwater of a house up in the hills. But the way this wealth barely concealed the poverty and structural racism present there, too, still stuck with us.

"My partner's parents bought this house when the neighborhood was still *so bad*," the acquaintance we visited in the hills had said, pale hands spread wide. Then she talked about teaching back in New York City and her fear of being stalked by one of her students, who was Black and working class and came to her office hours to discuss a grade. It was a balmy night. Earlier that day we turned down a street and found ourselves in one of the tent cities spread across LA. Now, we were at this miserable dinner party, sitting outside as we figured out how to excuse ourselves, drinking natural wine and staring at the twinkling yellow Christmas lights on the houses nearby.

When I saw *Scream* as a teenager, I watched until I could internalize its subjects as something to aspire toward, until the me of Elizabeth City was gone completely. I would be on the better coast and I would be a better me, freed from the violence of my de facto hometown. I dreamed of a life both Valley Girl and not, popular but sardonic, anchored in this place that had only been recognized by the US as part of its empire for a hundred years or so. I saw rows of houses identical in their splendor, imagining myself in each one, uncanny in the light of finally getting what I desired. How greedy, how limited my imagination. As I watched the movie, I emptied myself out, and when I kept watching, I watched until I was full, not realizing the thing I was trying to escape was me all along.

What does it mean to dream of something without even realizing it had been fed to you? California was different, I thought, until we visited, and I saw it wasn't. For my whole life, built up by movies like *Scream*, I saw the state as a place of escape, a home for better people with better problems than the ones in Elizabeth City. But the whole trip had been a wash; similar in everything but climate, it had barely been a trip at all. Instead, as our jet finally taxied off the runway to head back to New York, here is what I saw: a palm tree. The lights sparkling in the hills. The same petty supremacies as everywhere else. I saw my home.

In high school, I was lonely and sad and thought my loneliness and sadness were caused by the small town I lived in. I held on with certainty to the belief that once I escaped to a city or maybe even the West Coast, my sadness would cease. Well-liked and cosmopolitan, I would bask in the glow of a California sun, tell jokes while flipping my hair effortlessly over a shoulder. My bangs would be perfect and I'd be loved.

But I wasn't without friends; almost my whole time in Elizabeth City was spent around others. The loneliness was caused in part by my refusal to talk about why I was lonely—unnamed desires, a deeper discomfort with my body I hadn't yet learned to name. Elizabeth City hurt me, but mainly I was already hurt and passed that blame onto the city proper. I watched *Scream* until I could quote the words and with every line, every viewing, I tried to etch away the parts of my home I hated the most: the museum, the flooded sidewalks, the education system. But those were a part of me, too; as much as I felt I was hurt by the city, I was made by it as well. *Scream* is filled with wisecracks, but humor only takes you so far. Regardless of how hard I tried, I couldn't leave the South behind.

Swamps are known for keeping their secrets. The inner parts of me, the ones I tried to shed until the protests reminded me of them again, were still very much a swamp, teeming and beautiful, waiting, just waiting, to be found again. They were like my city, holding its secrets with care and love and community—and violence—just beneath the waterline.

3.

The killer of the movie, Ghostface, literally has a white mask for a face—one last irony in a film laden with them. The mask reveals what's beneath. The whiteness runs through.

I waited for weeks for a push alert about what would happen to Andrew Brown Jr.'s killers. Finally, I started searching myself, digging through articles from smaller newspapers weeks old at that point. In June, I discovered, the district attorney—who worked closely with the police officers involved in Brown's killing—had ruled his death as justified. Even before that decision, media presence in Elizabeth City was waning; as the protests progressed throughout the month, footage broadcasted nationally less and less frequently. Currently, the state still refuses to release the bodycam footage of the murder, and I barely hear anyone not connected to Elizabeth City talking about what happened to Andrew Brown Jr.

As the months went on, I rewatched the videos of protestors marching down the center streets of my town again and again. I read through takes online on the importance of rural Black communities, saw people I knew outside of North Carolina say Elizabeth City's name for the first time. And then I saw them stop paying attention. In the wake of the movement awakening there, I felt shame at my shame toward Elizabeth City. But I also felt angry: There, the reporters descended like tourists, too. They said *this city is in a crisis* and left it still in crisis. They did exactly what I did, but on an even more compressed scale—whiteness dictating whose stories get told and how, who gets abandoned, who is taught they don't owe anything to the place that reared them. I, after all, left, just like they did. This abandonment and exploitation is echoed in *Scream*, too: When the murders start happening, reporters, including Gale, descend on the town for scoops, and then, when things start to die down, disappear. In an inspired joke, throughout the rest of the series, every time a new murder happens, Gale reappears, apologizes for exploiting survivors' pain the previous time, and does it all over again. As escapist as *Scream* is, in at least one way it reflected a truth.

Life doesn't provide neat or easy resolutions to problems, but we weren't talking about life when the protests began. We were talking about justice, and justice's demands are spoken in a language clearer and more immediate than life's. The surviving family wanted the responsible parties to face charges for Andrew Brown Jr.'s murder. They wanted the segregation of the place to cease being enforced in the violent way it was. They wanted the police to stop. After the protests started, I thought a reckoning about the rural South and the need for greater equity would happen on a larger scale. Elizabeth City, I thought, would be talked about for longer than it was, and the classism and segregation of the place would finally be laid out, the museums revised to reflect the true history of the town. But once a month had passed, another police murder happened in a larger town, and out-of-towners resumed ignoring Elizabeth City. Most didn't even report about the bodycams or the verdict. They just appeared at a march, took pictures, and left again.

Even though I grew up unfamiliar with the suburbs, my town operated under the same logic. Here were the big houses my friends lived in. Here was the confidence they held to make the town into something appealing to themselves. Here was the result of their work: a fully segregated city and a series of ruins, the fitness center and the rusty water tower and the gnarled shipping yard, the seat of the town's power a century ago. And here I was: swallowing it all like I did everything that was fed to me, resentful but buying the bigger picture. It took a man in my hometown's murder for me to even fully realize how wrong I had been. I wasn't merely an oppressed queer victim in my hometown: I was one of the beneficiaries of the place, too. I dreamed of California, fantasized of escape. I left because I always knew that I could.

I was sixteen when the girl in the big white house and I kissed each other in the abandoned fitness center. I was home for the summer from the residential school I lived in, and the center was a fifteen-minute walk from our houses. Still, we biked, tees sticking slightly to our skins in the thick late-summer air. Heading up the waterfront in the opposite direction from the museum, we passed the wealthiest homes in the city, columned and tree-lined; we passed her place and before that, a few blocks inland, we passed mine. I thought there was a significant difference between us, but we were still within a ten-minute walk from each other, essentially in the same neighborhood.

We parked our bikes at a collapsed pier, laid them down in the grass by splintery fingers of the boardwalk. Holding hands, the girl and I walked up to the flooded, algae-soaked pool, the spiderwebbed broken shards of glass by the fitness center's entrance. We leaned our bodies against an overhanging bit of roof. "I've never done this before," she said, and I didn't know what she meant—kissed a queer? broke into an old building?—so I said nothing. The sun was setting and the river, as it did every night, turned a roiling pink, almost the same color as our flushed cheeks.

And then, suddenly, she was several inches away. We looked into each other's eyes and hers fluttered shut and so did mine. Several seconds later she pulled away. "Okay," she whispered, and we stared out at the water, shadows from the wrecked fitness center almost touching the crimson wavelets. The big green box of the museum was almost visible through the tree lines. I had been in this town for eight years and was about to leave it for good. As we settled down on the grassy concrete, our hands brushed against each other, holding each other quietly in the deepening dark.

Eventually, night would fall, and we'd turn around, shivering as the breeze pricked our damp skin. She'd put a light jacket over my shoulders and we'd walk back to our bikes, not realizing we wouldn't talk about any of what had happened again.

"You like scary movies . . . have you seen *Scream*?" she had asked. "It's not like these other films . . . it's funny. I think you'd like it."

The thing about *Scream* is that it's a movie disguised as a dream. The characters in it are comfortable in their skins, because they can be, because the writer perhaps couldn't and then could. It's a movie about identity, even though it doesn't know it is. But that's every movie. If you grow up white but not rich, Southern but not *Southern*, every piece of popular culture tells you you're better than what you came from. I swallowed the message because I wanted to, but also because it was made for me. I had my own delusions about myself, and *Scream* offered a way to envy and identify at the same time. I denied so much about my childhood, and *Scream*, a movie where white children stab each other over and over again because of their own inability to deal with their pasts, was the perfect canvas for that denial. It would be for anyone. It would be for anyone like me.

The girl and I would keep biking further into the night, past the mansions and private boats and cypress trees, the flooded streets and cemeteries and murals, the big brick public housing complex right by the boardwalk that we always glanced over and never looked at directly. I wouldn't reckon with any of the town for years, but for now, there we would be: Two blond girls, feeling the pull of escape, dreaming of being anywhere else—our plans for the future unspoken and spread out wide ahead of us. Pedaling slowly across the town, our pale skin lit only by the glow of the streetlights, the girl and I looked almost identical.

II.

Oh yes—there will be blood.

—**JIGSAW,** *SAW II*

War on Terror

1.

When the Iraq War started, we still had autumns; by October they were lush things, leaves ragged in violent reds and golds. I spent most of that first year at the end of elementary school at my friend Morgan's house—sidewinding my bike, a bright red Dr Pepper 18-speed I won in a lottery at our local Taco Bell, past the cracked-open sidewalks of downtown and the squat recruiting office with its sun-bleached Army Strong poster in the window.

We had a ritual, albeit an unspoken one. When I arrived, Morgan would be playing *Call of Duty* or another shoot-em-up. I'd sit in silence next to him, occasionally squealing at headshots or fumbling the controller when he passed it my way. Once he cleared a level, he'd turn off his dusty Xbox and we'd watch movies with only slight supervision. His dad worked late at the base most days and his stepmom was rarely home. On screen, arteries gushed open and ligaments bent back until they snapped like wishbones, and in the world outside there were still talks of deployed parents being home by Christmas. I had never seen hard-R horror films before, and he relished showing them to me. Someone he could teach and occasionally roughhouse, an accessory for his own interests. I was his girl before I even knew what that meant.

That fall, torture was in the air—in the commercials, TV shows, movies, splattered across *Fear Factor* and *The Texas Chainsaw Massacre* remake I wouldn't see until twenty years later, the Saw films and every other movie we did watch. It was in the soil. You couldn't not see it, even from within us, the invading country. Apologias for misconduct had already started to emanate from the *New York Times*, politicians, military leaders, whoever, excusing whatever had just happened and whatever would happen next. The president declared "Mission Accomplished" and then sent more troops out. It was a year before the first of the American torture scandals would break, and the culture of the time—camo-filled blockbusters, heroic Americans, smeary torture films—prepared Americans for our own complicity.

I didn't know any of this then, though. Mainly, I knew movies and longed for intimacy with others through the movies we watched. They reflected the war, too, and maybe on some level that's why Morgan chose them, but I didn't think about that, either. If you care enough about a person, after all, you can ignore almost any belief they hold. If you're devoted enough, a friend and a lover are nearly the same thing.

The first time I was beaten that I can remember was in kindergarten. It was on a playdate with a friend who saw in me something that drove him to assert a particular kind of dominance. His name was Jimmy, and he lived with his elderly parents in a small home littered with Lego bricks at the end of a long gravel road. Jimmy clambered on my back and rode me like a horse, kicking my sides if I didn't go fast enough. He dropped a cat on me from his second-floor landing. He scratched my arms and slapped me across the face, and I would take it but eventually push him off every time. His mother slept through or ignored all this, as I remember. Maybe I don't remember. I was barely present in my body for most of it.

When I knew Jimmy, I lived in Pennsylvania, the first state we moved to after the Virgin Islands: 2000 and a machinist's town, working class and gray. My parents worked as contingent faculty at the Catholic college down the road from our house, bay-windowed but right next to subsidized housing. Jimmy's home, in contrast, was almost a trailer, and I spent whole days there. I didn't tell anyone about how he hurt me during our time together, because I thought that was what it was to be intimate with anyone: punishment tempering closeness. I thought if someone shared physical space, then emotional space was guaranteed as well, regardless of what they did to me. For years afterward, I invited people into my life who hurt me again and again. We would watch things together. I would not remember any of it.

I met Morgan two years after Jimmy, the summer I moved to Elizabeth City. I was watching Scooby-Doo cartoons at the fitness center by the waterfront—the one that Hurricane Isabel would wreck the following year—when he walked up. Towel hung over a tanned hand, he sat next to me in silence. Once the episode was over, he looked at me and smiled slightly. "I'm Morgan," he said, and left.

We didn't talk much over the next year, as I was in third grade and he in fourth, but since we were both within walking distance of the fitness center, we passed each other on the sidewalk periodically. We'd chat briefly whenever we did and my heart would spring. When I skipped a grade the following year, though, we had homeroom together and started seeing each other more. Then, at some point, we were watching movies almost every weekend—his movies, violent ones.

Before fifth grade, I watched spooky movies, but not horror films. I loved the quiet melancholy of an old black-and-white werewolf film or the Halloween specials of sitcoms, the ordinary rhythm of jokes punctured by a Dracula or Frankenstein leering in the background. But when I entered fifth grade halfway through the school year, I started trying to adapt myself to the whims of the new crowd of people I was around, finding more elaborate ways to disentangle myself from my flesh. No: I tried to adapt myself to Morgan. He loved extreme films—messy, tit-filled, gory bloodbaths. So I grew to love them, too, or at least tried to. After all, we were friends; this was what friends did.

The horror films of the early 2000s were unusually violent and unusually prolonged in their violence. Heads got squashed, teeth pulled out. Bones were broken in places we didn't even think of. I hated these films, but I liked Morgan, so we kept watching. Every Saw or Final Destination movie. *Hostel*. *Turistas*. *House of Wax*. In them, we watched Americans get tortured—but, more specifically, we watched women get tortured. The violence they endured was sexualized—and as the violence was of course nonconsensual, the nonconsensuality was sexualized as well. Two blonds in broken tanning booths, their flesh blistering open to their screams in *Final Destination 3*. T-shirts, made to promote *House of Wax*, saying "See Paris [Hilton] die." The poster to *Turistas* on the wall directly above Morgan's bed, a bikinied woman's headless body leaking blood onto the beach stretching out beneath her.

In the outside world, violence continued as well. Every day, it seemed, another grim update about what happened abroad flashed onto our TVs. Morgan's father was Coast Guard, but there was talk about even him being deployed. But we were in a military town, so outside the regular schedule of deployments, we didn't talk about what was going on. Yellow ribbons bloomed on the backs of half the cars in Elizabeth City. And despite my disgust at these movies—I didn't see the point of seeing more violence, as it was already everywhere we looked—I'd shriek and laugh through every one, to his annoyance. This still happens. When I get scared, I start to giggle.

Morgan and I didn't talk about the war, in part because I was against it and I knew, on some level, he wasn't. I already learned to hold parts of myself—my hatred of the war despite being in a military town and absorbing a military town's propaganda, my own inchoate otherness—secret. No one in town talked about the war, actually, unless you count the empty rah-rah patriotism already inculcated in us with every morning announcement, pledge of allegiance, JROTC pep rally. Anti-war protests bloomed across the country, at the time historicized as the biggest in world history, but I didn't see any touch home in Elizabeth City. It was a Coast Guard town, and the war created the only jobs there. It's no wonder the country didn't need a draft. Economics took care of that.

In the meanwhile, the movies twittered on. In Morgan's favorite film, *Final Destination 3*, which came out in 2006, well into the war, we see a car's engine shred through the back of a man's skull. We see a roller coaster full of people run off the tracks. We see another man bellow, "Fuck death," right before his BowFlex breaks and the free weights crush his head apart. That was Morgan's favorite scene; while his dad conducted physicals at the Coast Guard base, we slipped the DVD back into his small TV at home, watched the man's skull explode in a cloud of blood and bone again and again.

Several months later, for his birthday (a Cancer!) I bought Morgan the novelizations of the Final Destination movies—cheap mass-market paperbacks I tracked down on Amazon, some repeating the plots of the films and some featuring new characters: Jessica Golden, a hard-rocking punk singer; Danny King, a high schooler who already has his own motorcycle; Patti Fuller, a journalist. I wrapped the books in butcher paper and tied a thin, sloppy bow on front with a ribbon I took from my parents' Christmas supplies in the attic. Then, I drew a tiny heart in the corner. We hadn't really gotten each other presents before, but I thought about it for weeks beforehand and was sure Morgan would love it.

When I handed him the small package after school, Morgan looked at me with confusion and I immediately knew I had made a mistake. "Thanks, I guess," he said. "You didn't have to do this."

He shoved the books in his backpack and slung it over his shoulder and hopped onto the bus ahead of me. We didn't sit together. My gut churned the whole ride home. When he hopped off the bus, he didn't say bye.

In 2006, I still thought that if I gave enough parts of myself away to people, I would get close to them. When we watched *Final Destination 3* for the first time, Morgan and I were upstairs, and in that moment, I thought we were close. There I was, my body resisting the urge to splay sideways against his body, to wrap his arm around my arm. There we were, the movie blaring on. We were good friends, which meant after we watched the movie, we rewatched the scene he most loved again, squealing as the weights pulped open the man's head on screen. Then rewind. Then collide again. Then collide again. Then he turned the film off, pulling out the Xbox.

"You can stay," he said casually. We were good friends, so I curled onto a pillow on his bed and laid my head as close as I could to him. We were good friends, so I didn't say anything despite the roiling inside of me to both get closer and get away. Onscreen, he mowed down dozens of people with a submachine gun. He threw a grenade and it fuzzed out the cheap TV speakers. His arm almost brushed mine. When I watched the movie again, just a few months ago, it felt surprisingly like a comfort, even though I hated it at the time.

2.

The movies were all about torture because everything was. For more than three years, Morgan and I watched Americans being hurt the same way our country hurt others in prison camps abroad, hoods draped over the faces of battered teenagers who were just trying to listen to Hoobastank. No one could talk about the torture because talking about it would mean admitting the violence the US was doing, our complicity in it as citizenry. So instead, we had the movies talk for us. Every one of the films I watched with Morgan reflected a guilt unacknowledgeable without confronting us; so there they sat unconfronted, growing more and more elaborate in their gore.

I'm not the first to make this connection, tying the domestic torture of, say, *Saw* to the acts done abroad. As far back as 2006, *New York* magazine film critic David Edelstein wrote about the connection between the two, framing horror movies as a genre of "inherent sadism," especially post-9/11. "Torture porn," he called these movies, and how neat a phrase it was in its petty imagination—expressing a distaste for the films and a distaste for sex itself in equal measure. A bear trap, ripping apart a jaw. A set of breasts bouncing in the sunset. It wasn't porn that was the problem, though, nor was it the torture and misogyny in the movies; it was what was continuing beyond. In Edelstein's condemnation of these "viciously nihilistic" movies, he doesn't even acknowledge the difference in scale between watching simulated violence on screen and perpetuating it. The two are fundamentally incomparable. "It might be true that the United States has lost its moral compass," scholar Aaron Michael Kerner writes in his 2015 book *Torture Porn in the Wake of 9/11*, critiquing Edelstein's framing, "but it is not because of torture porn but rather because we torture."

In addition to the Coast Guard base, Blackwater headquarters were thirty minutes outside of Elizabeth City. For the four years before what people called the "incident"—the mass murder of twenty Iraqi civilians, and the maiming of another seventeen—occurred, the company's logos—a bear paw encircled by a hunting sight—dotted the hoodies in the cafeteria line at my high school. When the news of the massacre broke in 2007 and the company's contract abroad was revoked, I went into school and saw a sea of chests, pawprinted and crosshaired in solidarity.

Torture exists, conveniently, in a space of deniable death: a mercy, ostensibly, in its reluctance to kill. Because of this, torture is sometimes de-emphasized in discussions of war's aftermath; in my own hometown, the murders that Blackwater guards carried out were far more heavily discussed than the maimings. The scholar Jasbir K. Puar critiques this framing of torture as a lesser evil in her 2017 book about the occupation of Palestine, *The Right to Maim*. It's not death that's the most significant violence, she argues, but this refusal to allow death. This is in part so insidious because wars are described first in terms of bodies lost, not larger damages done. An injured civilian—or even an injured soldier—is less visible to the liberal gaze than a dead one. "Maiming," Puar writes, "evades the optic of collateral damage," and through that maiming goes undiscussed. The right for an occupying military to maim, she argues, replaces the right to kill. Deployment after deployment after deployment of troops entered Iraq and Afghanistan during my childhood and apart from Abu Ghraib and Guantanamo, only the deaths—and then, only the spectacular deaths—were discussed. Maiming slunk by, existing as a slow death, a deniable death, a death that wouldn't even happen until years later, maybe even after the troops finally pulled out and the ruin left behind did its job.

In 2007, I was jumped by a student in eighth grade art class, skin blossoming open in little spurts of blood under a spray of fists, and afterward, a teacher laughed and said I deserved it for looking too much like a girl. The student's dad was Army, or maybe a private contractor; she wore a Blackwater hoodie like many other kids at school, delicate spiderwebs of freckles under her eyes. Her father surely tortured at least one person there—if not through what he did, then what he left behind. He did, like everyone else in our town, what he was sent there to do.

After being jumped, I was taken into the principal's office, a thin cube tucked away in a labyrinth of beige hallways. The principal furrowed her brow at me. "Do you want me to suspend you, too?" she asked. "It would probably be easier for you if your classmates thought the fight was reciprocated."

We were in early spring; several months earlier, the theater in town showed *Saw IV*. Since then, another troop surge had come and went, and I had been beaten twice. I chose suspension and was served three days out of school.

After my suspension, my father began taking me out to the garage, tumbler of wine in hand, to where he had strung up an old carpet tied together with thick twine and hanging cocksure from the rafters. "I want you to punch until it hurts," he said. Turning to face me, he put a leg forward and slugged me until I started hitting back. Then, he turned me to face the carpet and started counting punches until I couldn't punch anymore.

"We're doing this every night," my father said, "until you can fight." Then, almost as an afterthought he added: "We'll make a man out of you."

Maiming can be physical, but it can be emotional as well; Puar focuses as much on psychological damage as she does bodily damage. One of the cruelties of American war policy is that the ripples of physical damage so often spread out emotionally to a much wider set of people. A bomb goes off and hurts a man; he loses a limb but also a chronic fear of what happened has set into him. Perhaps it sets into his children, too. If they survive, their fear carries on, even if they don't name it, long after the troops have left.

Or perhaps: A soldier signs up to work for Blackwater. He is told to kill and to hurt, and he does so. Maybe he's been told to do that his whole life. He is gone most of the year, and abroad turns his homesickness and cravings into a more explicit form of violence. He was trained to do this, and he does it well. Then he gets home, and the violence is still there. What does he teach his children? What do they dole out in return?

Growing up, I was willowy and femme, hair tangling into thick snares. I was tired of being treated with disgust or turned into a receptacle for other's sexuality. I was tired of being told I needed to fight, needed to be a *better man*, whatever that meant. Instead, I longed to strip everything of myself, scrub my pinked flesh with steel wool until I was a bright blank slate. But intentions don't mean anything if you're living under someone else's rules, so regardless of what I wanted, there I was in the garage, serving punch after punch as the war roiled on.

Here's the broken core of the thing, the disjuncture between what I'm writing toward and my difficulty in saying it. There are two violences here, that of the empire and that of its denizens, and they are asymmetric violences, and different ones. But they are linked. One reflects another: The lessons of a militarized society become internal for everyone in that society. That's why it's broken. The violences: They can break you, and then you break someone else, even if in a more minor way at home than abroad—even if in a way that doesn't alleviate or justify what *was* done abroad.

I was broken, too, although I didn't know it yet. Throughout the whole war, I kept waking from a constant nightmare: I was playing with Jimmy again, hands tugging back my hair and scraping my back, but instead of dropping a cat on me or lowering me on all fours, he had me sit down and pried open my jaw. Then, slowly, he inserted something into my mouth that was soft and fleshy and pressed it to the back of my throat until finally I started to choke.

I last spent time with Morgan at a party in another friend's attic, a crowd of sweaty boys heaped onto a sagging gingham mattress on the floor. It was the summer. Empty cans of Mountain Dew were strewn around the room. Somehow, I hadn't seen him in months. I nodded at him, then everyone else, as I walked into the room. Then, our eyes locked briefly.

"What are you looking at, faggot?" he said.

I felt my stomach sink, the sharp taste of copper in my mouth. I didn't say anything, but inside rose something quiet and panging. I stayed at the party just another thirty minutes and on the way home told myself nothing was wrong.

That fall we entered high school; I ran cross country, then track, and made varsity in both of them. "I've never seen a runner so devoted," the coach said, and I *was* devoted, but only to the potential for my body to muscle away from the things that wanted to harm it. I told myself I was building a life more generous, more kind than the films I had seen, but separate from the catharsis of their violence, I had nothing: I ran. I punched the bag in the garage. I hit back. I still looked like a girl but concealed every other type of difference into a blur.

One day I heard over lunch that Morgan had signed up for the school's JROTC program, and later that day as I ran laps, I saw his loose curls poking out from under his tightly creased garrison cap. My hair flopped over my eyes, so I caught glimpses of him as through a very slow strobe light, interrupted every few seconds by a sweep of tangled blond. But through this I still saw him looking at me, then look away.

That fall I started to plan my escape from Elizabeth City. It was a military town full of cruel military people; I didn't want anything to do with it. I applied to a school far away from my current school, a free residential one for students talented in science or math. I was average at both but tested well and knew this could guarantee me admission if I wanted it enough. The recruiter was a tall man with gray-blue eyes like mine. With my own pedigree—professor parents, good grades—I had been scouted as sure as Morgan was. "You'll be welcome here," the recruiter told me.

As I walked down the hallway to hand in my application, I thought briefly about my former friend. I paused, and then started walking faster. There was nothing left for me in Elizabeth City, so I would find something elsewhere. I would be welcomed, I thought. I would be held. I would be free. Barack Obama was about to be elected. Abroad, the war would continue.

"Fuck death," bellowed the man lifting weights in *Final Destination 3*, and as we watched the first time, we both tensed on the bed like there was anywhere else we'd rather be.

3.

When I was twenty-two and living in Brooklyn, I got stoned with Danny, a friend who was in love with me. We giggled together, twined our hands gently around each other's, and ran outside to the park, reveling in the light breeze interrupting the mid-July heat. We had just watched *Sleepaway Camp*, a movie about a trans woman serial killer, screeching at the full-frontal reveal of her at the end. I loved the movie, even though I didn't tell Danny; something about the film, with its yearning young trans protagonist flinching at every implied violence she sees, penetrated me. I couldn't say that, though. The movie was stupid and we were high, more focused on making each other laugh than anything else. Years later on that same futon they would bend their neck back and I, as if commanded, would trace a hand around their frizzy bangs as we slowly kissed.

We dated for eight months. Danny kissed clumsily, and they fucked even clumsier. Elbows knocked together and fingers snared in hair, but we'd laugh about it together. They refused to bottom but didn't know how to top, so we remained in an awkward limbo the whole time, a messy blur of limbs and contradicting desires: I wanted to fuck whereas they didn't know what they wanted. No, that's not true: They wanted me. I wanted pleasure but beyond that, *I* was the confused one, and the warmth of their desire both brought me in and frightened me.

When we started to fuck, I responded because I felt, as good as their intentions were, that it was what I was supposed to do. But by the third time we had sex, I fell into a familiar pattern, absence cresting swift as a wave over my body and numbing everything. Suddenly, I wasn't in their twin-size bed. Instead, I was a child again. No, I was in high school. I was at the residential school. It was senior year and I was sixteen.

Before my Chinese exam that year, a boy had tried to hit me.

Actually, he had called me a faggot, and it felt like a hit. Actually, he had called me a faggot the previous day, but he looked at me with a smirk over a forkful of mashed potato, and I knew it would happen again. So I had vaulted over a table, pinned him to a brick column in the cafeteria and, like my father taught me, beat him until his face was beestung pink and purple. It was the first time I really hit someone else, and he whimpered slightly with each blow.

As I punched the boy in the cafeteria, I remembered it, and then tried to forget it again: Jimmy, holding my hair back. Jimmy, taking something and putting it in my mouth. I still don't know if it actually happened or was just the subtext of our interactions becoming concrete in my imagination, but I'm not sure there's a significant difference between the two. If you think something is true, I thought, part of it must be. The image bounced around again and again in my head, and in my memory every time he pulled my hair and entered my mouth, I would start to laugh.

When I knew Jimmy, the war hadn't started, but it would soon. Jimmy's parents weren't military, or maybe they were; they weren't home, regardless. He loved to watch loud cartoons with lots of fighting, so he was influenced by what was in the air. A flicker of TV, a flash of pink. And during the commercial breaks, a trailer for a horror movie coming out on VHS. A plane crash. A premonition of death. Him pulling my head back, hair yanked almost off the head. Something inside me broke then although it took me years to realize it, and in the meanwhile, the TV kept droning on, body after body maimed until nothing was left.

After what felt like hours in the cafeteria, I stepped away, panting with effort. My fists were red, and so was the boy's face. "Okay, man," he mumbled, eyes darting nervously around the cafeteria to find someone to help him. No one was willing to, and his eyes swelled with fear. He had no one. Bruised, he crept out of the cafeteria, skipping classes until the swelling went down.

There's a joy in violence, too, although it's an awful, rending joy. I loved myself as I stepped away, felt strong and powerful in my body. Finally, I thought, I was a man. Then I threw up.

"Are you there?" Danny asked, mouth ever so slightly wet, and there I was again, and they had stopped touching me, our clothes tangled and half removed on the futon. I tried to speak but my throat closed up and my face rutted with tears. "Hush," they said, and their hand awkwardly hovered over me until I grabbed it and curled into their warmth as, gradually, it passed.

We tried to talk about what happened, but I think they were scared by it, the suddenness with which I vacated my body. We stopped fucking just weeks after that, and when we saw each other as friends next it was awkward, strained, like something happened between us that left our tongues unable to find the words.

"I can't keep doing this," they said. "I don't even think I can see you as a friend. It's too weird." And then we were done completely, the great span of what happened stretched out between us.

The need to watch violent horror movies, I suspect, is rooted to the preponderance of violence already in a life. When I was sexualized the first time, this sort of violence became normalized in me. I grew to expect it. But I never felt comfortable around it. Watching other bodies marked for violence gave me a way to enter that comfort, as discomfited as that has made me since. With Morgan, I saw a wrecked body suspended in barbed wire, a nail gun fire again and again through a head. With Danny, I saw a trans woman shoot arrows into the neck of her tormentor. I wasn't the only one learning to feel through fake violence. It was no quirk of timing that Morgan and I got close through watching scary movies; as the country lurched to a war that still hasn't ended, *Final Destination 3* grossed more than any Final Destination before it. Every movie with violent death was making more money than the last, even as the news refused to show coffins.

The horror makeup artist Tom Savini, who jump-started the increase in gore and torture in American scary movies with his special-effects work in the eighties, served as a combat photographer with the military in Vietnam. That, he says, is why his work was so realistic: He pulled the images directly from his memory. A massacre became a zombie bisected by a helicopter in *Dawn of the Dead* became a bloated corpse in *Creepshow* became a scalped bloodied woman in *Maniac*. Setting a precedent, war reproduced in the films, the latter not even present without the former: New tools of murder became integrated, reflected in simulation. These new, bloody, extreme films kept getting grimier and more creative in their kills until eventually they found themselves in the 2000s, with what became torture porn.

Sleepaway Camp, the movie I watched with Danny, was initially conceived as a rip-off of *Friday the 13th*, Savini's most famous film. A scene where a counselor is pierced with an arrow in *Sleepaway Camp* is a pale, bloodless echo of a deeper-crimson-covered tableau in *Friday*. Even their settings, a melancholy set of summer camps, are the same, as are the murderers: Women crazed with loss, trying to build lives for themselves through the limited violence they have access to.

Ultimately, *Sleepaway Camp* is an imitation of an imitation of a trauma. I fell in love while watching it with Danny despite its photocopied plot, or maybe because of it. It was delirious in its affect, all appropriated dusty ochres and fever dreams of campers mutilated. The movie was a war filtered until it couldn't even be seen anymore. Then, the new war came, and everything got remade, and more straight-to-DVD sequels to *Sleepaway Camp* were churned out, all sitting alongside the torture films in the horror aisle in Blockbuster, each movie for all the world indistinguishable from one other.

Throughout high school, as Morgan went through the JROTC program, his posture got straighter. His hair cropped shorter. He began to walk with more purpose and wore his uniform every Friday, crisp and deep blue. I watched him, and soon he started saying the same slurs as everyone else. Meanwhile, I ran. I hit. Although I didn't make the connection, I was transforming my body in the same way as he was—as if I wanted to be him. But I wasn't him. I was me. Our lives had been so intertwined that they almost shared the same root: the same movies, the same video games, the same tolerance to violence. But even though we were made by the same town, made by each other, we weren't each other. We were friends. And then we separated and were nothing.

Lying together in his bed one day in middle school, Morgan put on *Hatchet*, a movie where a bunch of teens are cut up in a swamp. We lived in a swamp. We weren't yet teens, but I could taste it coming, a future of bodies crooked against one another or gored in a blur of mortar and AK-47s overseas. Morgan's dad was away at the military base, and in bed with him I thought he'd never return. There I was—on his bed pulling the quilted cover around me, poster of *Turistas* peeling slightly off the wall, antiperspirant and musk in the air. My eyes widened. A head lopped off. Our hands darted away from each other. It was early 2008. I thought of what we might do and what we didn't, and inevitably, as the teens were mauled by the hatchet-wielding killer, I started to giggle. The news earlier that day said the war was going to end.

"Why are you laughing?" said Morgan, and as I looked at him, I didn't know how to say anything at all.

In war, the media of the 2000s told us, there is no love, no tenderness or intimacy; there's just violence. I don't know how much he was pressured by his father to enter JROTC, how much he was pressured by his peers to turn on me. He had a military dad in a military town; of course he saw a future with the military. He was biracial in the South; of course he grew up with violence, too. I don't actually remember the beginning of the war, but in some ways that's the point: As a war stretches on to forever, the terms of its origin become more and more muddied. Instead, it was there as backdrop, which is to say it was always there. Surely, he felt that, too.

At the time, I was scared Morgan would leave to fight as well, take one of the military planes flying low and loud above Elizabeth City and enact the violence and maiming he had been trained to. But I was also scared he would leave *me*. I didn't say any of this to him either; instead, I just smiled softly. I was in love with Morgan, and if I'm being honest, as our hands lay next to each other on the blanket, fingers almost touching, I don't remember who pulled away first.

4.

PTSD received its first diagnosis in soldiers; the *T* in the name refers originally to the trauma of war's legacy—which is to say, debility, death, maiming, witnessing. Even the language we have to name trauma is rooted in systems of war, which is why I'm so reluctant to use that language to describe what happened to me. First it was called shell shock, then combat fatigue, and finally, in the 1980s, settled into its current name. The diagnosis, and its timeline, directly related to the aftermath of the Vietnam War.

But almost immediately the label was applied asymmetrically: focusing almost exclusively on Americans, the occupying force, and never on the occupied. War hurts, but it doesn't hurt everyone in the same way, or to the same extent; the limit of PTSD is how it collapses all violences into the same violence, with the same diagnostic response. Anything can be traumatizing, but they all have the same word to describe them, which means the language becomes diluted for those who need it most.

Jimmy was a child, which means, legally and logistically, he wasn't fully responsible for his actions. I don't even know if anything happened to him, although statistics say there was probably something. But after he did whatever he did to me, I couldn't be fully present with anyone. I pulled away from those who drew near, shut off when I should have been on. I taught myself to be hard, to not expect anything but disappointment from those I loved or wanted to love. These weren't difficult lessons to learn: They were the ones taught all through our town, echoed in the recruiting ads and military formations my classmates marched in during JROTC practice after school. They were even there on the track field, with its endless drills and the coach who told us "Again. Again. Again." with every lap. Even when I punched out the boy in the high school cafeteria, I floated slightly above my body, not myself, if I ever was.

Memory works two ways; while we remember what hurts us, it's easy to block out how we have hurt others. "It's not Vietnamese bodies I see in my nightmares," one veteran disclosed in a 2015 C-SPAN interview, "it's me."

With Morgan, I longed for our bodies to embrace, but I didn't remember until now my own distancing from him, even before he pulled away from me. With the boy in high school, I almost forgot how satisfied I felt after punching him; in Danny's bed, I just felt the fear at first, not the joy. Once I finally touched another body, I thought I could find myself in it, but even now I'm not being honest with what I remember. Person after person made space for me in their life, and I just continually shot back instead to the violence that made me: a bed, a hand across mine that I didn't want to want to touch, soft flesh pushing into a mouth, our military town and all that pumped out of it. The force of war is such that it's present in PTSD's language of diagnosis even now—terrorism and war both appear before *rape* in the American Psychiatric Association's definition of the sorts of trauma that contribute to the disorder. Growing up with what I won't call PTSD, I wanted to bond with others through intimacy, to shift myself through sheer force of will into someone who was whole. But we're never whole, at least those of us raised under the shadow of men or the military or the casual violence that pervades us. We're just here.

After Danny held me, I began to settle back into myself. Their blanket was covered with stars—can you imagine that? A twenty-eight-year-old with a star blanket?—and they draped it around my shoulders. Their breath brushed against my neck, sweet and slightly too hot, and when I flinched, they pulled back immediately. Maybe we can't reconcile what's been done to us and what we do to others in turn. Maybe intimacy can never be a salve for the larger impact of violence. It was 2018 and they said on the news the troops were being removed again, even though we didn't believe it. The summer-sticky evening breeze floated through the window.

Danny smiled at me even though we would separate soon, and in that moment—just for that moment—I felt safe and held and fully present in their arms. I turned to hold them back as I started to blur out once more. *I could love this person*, I thought. And then, everything started happening again, and I was gone.

Southern Fried

Here's the thing about beauty: It's painful. And for a while, I'd try to hide the pain. For the longest time, I'd tell people I loved art-house films as a way of making my own desires seem more palatable: the movies of Apichatpong Weerasethakul or Ingmar Bergman or Terrence Malick or any other director who specialized in long, winding, thoughtful shots and barely restrained emotions. I'd tell them they helped me see the splendor of the world around me, how their restraint helped me see myself. I do love them, and it's true that a part of me was found there. But of all the movies I've seen, I've found the most splendor in *The Texas Chain Saw Massacre*, discovered myself the most in it—a revving engine of a film, sick and quick and all deep reds. In fact, this is how it worked: First I loved it, and then I loved myself.

The title tends to turn people off. What they picture is something closer to the remake: a blunt object, a leering gaze, a body turned into an object to be fucked or cut up with nothing in-between. But what I saw in it was my home—and because of that, what I saw in it was a kind of care. And through that intimate pain—for care can be painful as well—we get back to beauty, too.

I first watched *The Texas Chain Saw Massacre* in high school during the brief window when full movies were uploaded to YouTube, the image 240p and broken up into six parts to circumvent the website's then fifteen-minute video limit. I lived at a residential school three and a half hours away from my parents and started watching it in my dorm room between second and third period, finishing the movie after chemistry lab. I was miserable at that high school, but it was a misery I couldn't even name yet. I didn't even think it was unique at that time to hate my body. Everyone, I thought, pictured themselves sliding into a lake and not coming out again. I watched the movie because it had been framed online as an endurance exercise; if I could endure *The Texas Chain Saw Massacre*, I thought, it would prepare me for life.

But what I didn't expect were the film's visuals, which even through digital grain shone bright. Fields of tall grasses rippled slowly in the breeze. A car rumbled down the highway, exhaust exhaling behind it like a ghost. And at the moment that Sally Hardesty, the movie's beleaguered protagonist, is held captive at the cannibal family's dinner table, grandfather preparing to hit her with a hammer, the film zooms in unexpectedly on one of her eyes flitting around in fear, her iris the most verdant green I'd ever seen.

I had been in North Carolina for just over nine years at that point, and I expected *The Texas Chain Saw Massacre*, with its rural cannibals and grindhouse title, to reaffirm my existing prejudices. The South was ugly, I thought; it looked ugly, and people acted ugly, and I wanted a film that would reflect that. I watched to endure it, but also to confirm what I already knew.

The Texas Chain Saw Massacre is short and straightforward, part of the reason I was able to finish the movie in just two chunks between classes. A group of hippies from the local college town set out to visit their grandfather's old property. They pick up a hitchhiker, who sets a picture of them on fire and slices at them with a knife; they kick the hitchhiker out of their van. They stop at a gas station to fill up and have a brief conversation with the proprietor, who's also a barbecue cook; the man leers as they drive away. They visit their grandfather's house, and then slowly everyone drifts to the house behind their grandfather's, where a family of workers laid off from the local slaughterhouse live. The hitchhiker is there. A grandfather who looks centuries old is there. Leatherface, a six-foot-seven man in cowboy boots and a mask made out of human skin, is there. Eventually the gas station cook is there. Quickly, everyone but Sally dies, leaving her screaming and laughing alone, splattered in blood, in a flatbed truck speeding away from the house at dawn. It's over in just eighty-three minutes.

At the residential school, we looked at slides of pond water through multichambered microscopes donated by Duke University up the road. We picked apart frozen cat bodies, peeling the muscles on a leg back one by one to reveal the femur, then the tibia, the stiff ankle bones, the phalanges. It was a free school, built on the rundown grounds of a former hospital, and one that had been wiggled into the state university system: Our student IDs, we were told, could get us into any library or science lab we wanted access to. We were the pride of the state, the best it had to offer. I'd wake every morning to birdsong.

Because of its low budget, most of *The Texas Chain Saw Massacre* was shot with natural lighting, which is part of what lends an eerie prettiness to the surroundings: Their world, with its scrabble of brush and dust smeared everywhere and slowly setting sun, looks just like ours. A couple in their twenties gently pushes the long amber grasses to the side to explore a neighbor's house. House spiders weave webs, fibers shining in the afternoon light. At night things purple under dim moonlight, and in evening the film is heavy with sun, bright and sticky as a melting blood orange. Texas isn't North Carolina, but at that moment I started to see both as not just ugly but gorgeous as well, spread out and broad. There, the trees and low shrubs have seen everything. There, there's nothing that doesn't promise to bloom.

I entered the movie wanting to be scared because I dealt with my problems by being scared. Otherwise, I'd feel too needy, too vulnerable and exposed. But that which entrances us and frightens us is so often the same. I hated the South, feared being Southern myself even, but in *Chain Saw*, everyone talks with an accent—even the heroes. Everyone walks through the grasses, runs through hardscrabble Southern trees. It's not whether you're from the South or not that matters, the movie seemed to be saying: It's what you do with it, and how you or others are hurt despite it.

I don't know if these themes were intended. *The Texas Chain Saw Massacre* was a film notoriously shot on the fly; director Tobe Hooper stayed up all night shooting the last twenty minutes of the movie, and no one washed their clothes through the whole shoot because they couldn't afford second outfits and were scared of the clothes being stolen from the local laundromat. All the rotting animal parts in the film were real and by wrap day everyone was nauseous from the smell. The film couldn't even afford stunt people, so in a scene where Sally Hardesty jumps out a second-floor window, the script consultant pulled on a blond wig and actually did the jump herself, twisting an ankle in the process. I don't even know if the movie was intended to look as beautiful as it does; maybe its starkness just came from a budget constraint that aged especially well, in the same ways that the cheaply recorded folk albums from the '70s sound less dated now than the studio schmaltz a big budget could get you. In filming, it seems, there was little thinking involved; the whole movie instead just existed as an *experience*. When the shoot was over, the rumor goes, the crew made shirts that said, "I survived shooting Texas Chain Saw Massacre!"

Ultimately, I'm not interested in intention. I felt things watching the movie, and those I showed it to felt things, too. We talked about it afterward, everyone offering their different interpretations as to what *Chain Saw*—loud, intimate—was about. The movie was a gift to us, and our conversations afterward were a gift back.

With a girl from my MFA I would start dating just weeks after we watched the movie, *Chain Saw* became a film about animal rights abuses. We'd just shared a joint, wound up and electric with energy. "See?" I said, pointing to the shots of a slaughterhouse where the cannibal family used to work. "They're treating the humans like cattle."

With an ex I fell back in love with over the pandemic, it was a film about feminized labor, and even transness. Leatherface, the person who ostensibly does the killing in the family, is also the softest member. He wears masks made of human skin but covers them in eyeshadow and lipstick and is viciously bullied by his siblings for not fitting in to what they think a man should be.

"You like this face?" Leatherface's brother cries mockingly to Sally as she's held captive at the dinner table, and it's hard to say who he's making fun of more.

My partner Avery saw the film as being about disability and being different. There are two families in the movie, the killers and the killed, and both of them have disabled characters at their core. Franklin, Sally's brother who rides in a van with the rest of the victims, uses a wheelchair and is constantly berated by his peers. Leatherface, who doesn't even speak or show his face outside of a mask, appears to have some sort of developmental disability and is kicked and hit by his older brother as he whimpers in pain. In the film, anyone who can't keep up with the demands of an ableist society gets killed.

Maybe this wasn't the film's doing, but something changed in me the first time I watched it. I'd walk down the sun-dappled streets of Durham, where the residential school was—sometimes heading to my therapist's office, sometimes just walking to get a lavender milkshake from the malt shop on Broad Street—and pictured the plains and thatchy backwoods of Texas, a preemptive longing for where I already was starting to creep over me. Around me sprang tall reaching trees and bullfrogs. Cardinals and thrushes chirruped from telephone poles, sun-warmed cricks everywhere. From the instrument repair shop run out of a trailer off Broad, staticky country music drifted over the radio. I had spent nine years in North Carolina, and that was five years longer than anywhere else. The South, for better or for worse, was my home. *Chain Saw* felt like something emerging, fully formed, from a bog, and I was emerging, too—albeit much more slowly. And who hasn't felt nostalgia for a place because it was where they first realized who they truly were? Who hasn't found themselves in something they didn't even realize they were looking for?

Despite its beauty, *The Texas Chain Saw Massacre* is still an unrelentingly cruel movie. Leatherface spends the film's end in pain, accidentally chainsawing through his leg after his brother is killed by an 18-wheeler chasing Sally, blood splattering over everything. The twentysomething protagonists are menaced and turned into meat with alacrity. Even the heroes are cruel. Sally's brother Franklin is brilliant, funny, and anticipates everything that happens in the movie—but the other people in the van, the ones who die first, hate him.

"Franklin's no fun" goes the refrain, even though our introduction to Franklin is him being blown out of his wheelchair from the backdraft of a semi, tumbling down a steep hill into a ditch. Even though Franklin is dragged around to ancestral mansions with steep steps he can't get his wheelchair up and is left behind as his friends run off to go swimming (I can't help but think of our friend in LA in 2019, unable to navigate the sidewalks in her wheelchair). Early in the movie Franklin is cut by the deranged hitchhiker and is later sawed in half by Leatherface—the most violent death in the movie—and still everyone hates him, even the audience; I've read review after review about how insufferable and annoying Franklin is, although as far as I'm concerned, the only thing he's done wrong is exist in a world that refuses to make space for him.

When I first watched *Chain Saw*, I was in the midst of my second-most intense spate of self-harm. For months, I'd creep into the shared dormitory bathrooms at 2 or 3 a.m. to hit myself until I started crying and then hit myself more until I stopped feeling anything. I'd practice cruelty against myself that crept into a cruelty against others, too; a stiffened unapproachability, a studied distance intended to prevent anyone from getting too close.

When I set out to watch the movie, I wanted it to hurt like I hurt me. Horror movies were another way to punish, I believed at the time. But while the movie is punishing, it's unexpectedly beautiful, too. Of course the sudden rush of seeing *Chain Saw* in the compressed YouTube window pierced me. It showed me the care you can find when seeking out hurt—which is to say, again, that it showed me my home.

There are the marks that are left on us, and then there are the marks we leave on ourselves, and I'm still not sure if there's a difference between the two. The South shaped me, and the South hurt me, but that doesn't change the fact that I'm Southern and thus implicated in its own violence—raced and classed and sure as my own violence toward myself. Maybe there's no difference at all between the social ostracization I received in the South and my rage at the other Southerners stuck in my small town and finally the punches I started to dole out to myself—all were motivated, after all, by a refusal to see the beauty in a harsh and beautiful environment.

Until I turned seventeen, I treated the South with a smug superiority, one that cut me off from who I really was. Because I grew up there, the South left its sticky summery marks on me, and then once I rejected it, I left my marks on me, too, sure as a burn. I moved from rural North Carolina to urban North Carolina, and then I moved to New York—and gradually, in my moves, I refined my own cruelty as well.

The remake, which many people think of when they think about *Chain Saw*, contains none of this beauty. It came out one day before the United Nations affirmed, for the third time, the importance of US troops in Iraq and the duty of the rest of the West to contribute to the war as well. On TV, commercials for the 2003 movie aired between ones for dive-bombing jets, armed forces rappelling down a rock wall, desert fatigues. The film reflected all of that, MTV-style sheen slicked across the screen and dirty browns and tans running everywhere and gore filling every second. It opens with a hitchhiker who seems to have been sexually assaulted—blood running between her legs—blowing her brains out in the back of the main characters' van. Then, the film escalates to a menacing sheriff, or someone who claims to be a sheriff, licking his lips over her dead body with a necrophiliac longing. I tried watching the remake on Netflix years later with a friend I was fucking—a girl who whimpered during the scary parts, liked to be slapped, and walked with me to get ice cream after the first time we had sex—but I shut it off after thirty minutes. I couldn't bear any more. The compassion I loved in the original film was missing almost completely.

Of course, this extraction has only intensified. *Chain Saw* was remade again—or remade-cum-sequel'd—in January 2022. In it, like in every other one of the eight miserable sequels and remakes, splays of gore and pop nihilism replaced everything I loved in the original. A group of woke teens are massacred on a party bus. A woman's life is saved due to the Second Amendment, as she fires away at Leatherface with the shotgun she scorned earlier in the film. It's all reprehensible in a crypto-Republican way, but more than that it's boring. The militarization of the 2003 film had seeped through its following sequels and further reboots; the politics of torture and exploitation became the only thing to watch for. The war, in many ways, had never ended. The beauty was gone.

It's an old story at this point: Hollywood finds a film that's striking and decides it's striking for the wrong reason, and then capitalizes off that mistaken assumption. That was actually why my friend and I watched the 2003 film: We wanted to see if what we had just seen, the most recent one, was the nadir of the franchise. And it was, at the time, but there's always a lower level one can sink to. Despite this endless progression of worse and worse movies, though—and I don't doubt there will be more, worser movies to come—it doesn't take away from what I love about the original.

Yes, in the original movie the horrors are inescapable and indiscriminate; hurt people hurt people hurt people or whatever. And yes, in watching *Chain Saw*, I meant to hurt myself just like I did in the shared bathrooms at school. But even through the intensity, there's a generosity to the film—its lingering in the corners of the South; its richness of image and feeling; its dedication to the totality of its characters' emotions. I was dedicated to feeling, too, dedicated to beauty, although I didn't know it yet. The more time I spent with *Chain Saw* and with others, the more I loved it in its mess. And the more I loved it, the more I found myself.

At the end of the film, Sally is escaping on a speeding flat-bed truck. Her brother is dead, chainsawed out of his wheelchair by the only other disabled character in the movie. Her boyfriend is dead. Her friends are dead. But the movie doesn't end. As she's laughing in fear and relief, the film cuts to Leatherface, who, limping and illuminated in the rising sun, raises the chainsaw first to his side and then above his head and starts to pivot his body like a ballerina. Soon, he's fully pirouetting, hurt and angry and sad and confused himself. As the chainsaw brushes against the camera, the film cuts to black, and then finally it's over—nothing left but his pain and her relief and what they made together from both. I am seventeen, staring at my laptop in between classes. Someday I will stop hurting myself, but not yet. Someday I will learn to love everything I find gorgeous, including myself.

I don't believe that a film's legacy can really be defined by the remakes or sequels that come after it. I think anything you care about exists, at least partially, in the moment you first care about it. Maybe that's why I'd go on to watch the original *Chain Saw* with so many people I'd love. The interpretations of the film we shared were a way of sharing each other, letting one another in. Beauty can stun, too, and sometimes the only thing to do with that is to hold that complexity with others. There wasn't one way to view *Chain Saw*, after all; there were many—like a life. This is what was beautiful about it—life, the movies, art, whatever—the fact that it could be shared, endured, and held with others.

I loved *The Texas Chain Saw Massacre* before I loved myself. And maybe the two aren't related, but one did follow the other. But for now, I walk out of my dorm as the film begins to settle in me, a bruise from earlier sending out spiderwebs of shock through my body. As I leave the dorm building, I look at the state around me—greening leaves, rickety pines, kudzu creeping up the side of a building—and for the first time see it as something also beautiful, harsh and splendid and irreducible.

The croak of leaf-roller crickets starts up, and from a distance they almost sound like a chainsaw's hum. It's spring and I am seventeen, quad's grass tickling my ankles. I'm starting to realize that there are other ways of loving things besides holding them close, that there is a love in allowing others to love things, too. Soon, I'll scrub back to the beginning and press play again; I will leave the South and move to New York; I will gather round my exes and lovers and friends and in different apartments across the city and over Zoom we'll quiet and watch Leatherface's delicate, uninhibited dance, the roar of his tool. Together we'll talk about what it means to survive, find care in both the pain and survival together. In 2024, I'll watch it again with a new partner, and her face will glow with excitement by the end of the movie. "This is the South?" she'll say. "It's gorgeous."

In 2010, it's bright and yellow outside and the air smells like pine, and I'm starting to realize that everything about my life will have to change. The bruise throbs, and I wince, air sharp and cool as I inhale. Eventually I will learn to share that beauty, too, even though it'll be years still before I stop harming myself. Soon, the sun will set. But for now the light comes into me like birdsong. Someday, I will be free.

Cutting in Miniature

When I was working on my first book, in the long middle of it—after my father had died, but before I locked the manuscript in my desk drawer for months—I had a dream that stuck with me with violent viscerality.

In the dream, I went upstate to give myself more time to finish the collection of poetry I was working on about Lizzie Borden, the lesbian family-murderer. I paid for an Airbnb for six months and brought my reams of research materials with me, settling in the pine-dappled cabin I rented. It was so pretty: a mulchy long field of a yard, a burbling crick. Before I knew it, the six months were up. I locked my manuscript in my drawer and called my friends.

"I've finished my work," I said, "I need to tidy up, and then you can come celebrate with me."

I hung up the phone and began to clean, but as I swept, I noticed the bristles of the broom were dappled with crimson, leaving tiny red streaks on the floor. I went out to walk across the floorboards and my shoes squished out red. I washed a stack of dishes and saw a growing dark stain on the ceiling above the sink. I ran upstairs to the bedroom and there I found blankets bundled around something wet and large, the mattress underneath soaked like a sponge. Then, finally, I realized my home was filled to the brim with bloodied, rotten bodies.

I ran around trying to hide the gore-drenched corpses, but every time I put one away—chopped into bits in the trash can, crumpled in the pantry next to a Cuisinart—I found more. Finally, I went back to my writing room. When I opened the locked drawer I'd put the manuscript in, I saw jumbles of hands stacked to the top of the drawer, lopped off ragged and quick at the wrist. During those six months of dream time, I had not written a word, but instead killed and killed again.

I woke up and put the manuscript in a drawer, and, like in the dream, I closed the drawer and locked it. I didn't write again for almost six months.

In the dream and in real life, I wrote to distract myself from my nascent grief. It was 2017, and I thought if I wrote hard and far enough into my subject, I would spare myself the emotional collateral of my father's sudden passing. I wrote about Lizzie Borden, a woman who murdered her stepmother and father in the middle of the day at the turn of the twentieth century and got acquitted.

I hadn't seen any of the several movies about Lizzie Borden when I started the collection. My closest connection to Lizzie was a play I saw about her at the local playhouse when I was ten. I attended the play with my mother, and it spawned a miniature obsession; I spent weeks combing true crime forums for her trial documents, trying to make sense of a set of murders that terrified me deeply. When I started in on the poetry collection thirteen years later, I tried to figure out why I had been so haunted by Lizzie's story, the thin parallels between her life and my own. In writing, I focused on a father undoubtedly cruel to Lizzie Borden but who Lizzie seemed to love even despite this cruelty, until she killed him. I thought writing it could make sense of my own childhood and heal me from what my own father had imprinted on me.

I work, in many ways, in miniature. When writing, I make spreadsheet tables and draw diagrams to fit poems within. I adjust my Google Docs margins as small as I can and size down the font to nine- or eight-point and zoom in. I try to look as closely at something as I can until I can't look any longer, and I call that process revision. I cut and cut away until there are just slivers left. I slivered away over a whole unbearable spring and summer. Then, two years later, I published my ode to Lizzie and assumed my nightmares would cease.

But then the collection came out and the dreams didn't stop. By the two-year anniversary of its publication, Lizzie was half of what I thought about—both asleep and awake—crimson creviced into the floorboards and walls of a narrow slit of a home. So, I decided to physicalize this haunting: to make a crime scene of Lizzie Borden's home, a diorama. I thought if I captured my dream-fear into something material, I could trap it, hold it, and then hide it away.

Building a miniature crime scene to deal with these larger, accumulated fears wasn't my own idea; it was Frances Glessner Lee's. For the previous few years, I had been both fascinated and disgusted with the woman who trained the New Hampshire police in forensics during the middle of the twentieth century. The journalist Rachel Monroe writes extensively about Lee in her 2019 book *Savage Appetites*, calling her "a woman of intense focus . . . not particularly fond of [other] women," but what fascinated me the most about Lee were the elaborate dollhouses she built for her trainings. Inside one-tenth scale crime scenes, tiny mothers oven-asphyxiated in their ranch homes and doll men hung from floss-thin nooses in the barn.

Frances Glessner Lee was wealthy and lonely. As a younger woman, she had wanted to go to college for medicine but at her family's request had instead married the son of a former Confederate general, bearing three of his children. Growing up on Chicago's Millionaire's Row and marrying who she did, she was steeped in prejudice and money alike; her supplies to build the dollhouses were procured by her servants, not by her, and the models themselves were co-built by a team of artisans. Her victims appear to span a wide class range, but this doesn't necessarily reflect the diversity of her own social circle. To make her dollhouses, she scoured court transcripts, too.

Lee's background certainly explains her affinities with the police, how she viewed them as a solution to violent crime as opposed to another manifestation of it. You don't pour such detail into such models, models made specifically to educate, unless you respect the work of policing writ large. But in the dolls, which she crafted by hand in excruciating detail, I saw a kind of care as well, directed at something that so obviously terrified her. There was a deep intentionality behind them—the bright crimson of blood, the tiny shoelaces on their feet. Yes, I hated the ideology behind what Lee did, but I loved what she made: how delicate the dioramas were, how precise and skillful. In the work, I saw something to aspire to.

Before my dream, Lizzie's life was easy to write about because the excavation the project required had nothing to do with me. For most of 2017, I had plunged myself into research, even more so than I did when I was younger: corresponding with clerks to get scans of her inquest, lurking on forums, checking dozens of books out of the Brooklyn Public Library and scouring their works cited pages to find primary documents I may have overlooked. Lizzie was a Sunday school teacher, I learned. She went to Europe once, with her sister. She refused to move out of her town after her acquittal and was ostracized until her death—compounded by her semi-public relationships with women, most notably actress Nance O'Neil. The hatchet that Lizzie purportedly committed the murders with went missing from the police's evidence box shortly before the trial, so there was nothing explicitly linking her to the murders, even though there was no one else who really could have done it. She had fits of anger and melancholy frequently.

I wrote the book in the attic of the queer co-op I lived in, and despite the twenty-one people I shared a house with, the place got bone quiet at night. Before bed, I looked at photo after photo of Lizzie's rounded, soft-butch face and dreamed about what her nights were like. I wouldn't think about my father, who had just entered the hospital as I started to write. I wouldn't think of why I was drawn to these girls—her and Nell Cropsey and Samara Morgan from *The Ring*—who didn't seem long for this world. Lizzie had more power, but she was just as linked to death, and loss, as the others were. I would only think of her.

Two years later, I felt this same thrum of familiarity while making the miniature. In my own labor, I told myself, I was working to capture the accomplishment and grief Lizzie surely felt at the conclusion of her task, just as I'm sure Frances Glessner Lee felt catharsis building her models, too.

Perversely, being immersed in a murderer's life again was a welcome distraction from my lingering grief. Acquainted with the rhythms at this point, I began to research once more: first the grimy crime-scene photographs of her father, head meloned open on the fainting couch; then swatches of period-appropriate wallpaper and blood splatter analysis to simulate what being struck with a hatchet might look like on a ceramic doll. I bought metal rulers and thin sheets of plywood, modeling clay and dollhouse glue. I bid on eBay for the cheapest dollhouse accessories I could find, then cut them down and repainted them and built them back up for the house. I replaced a blurry portrait of some flowers with Andrew Borden's own crime scene photo, resting like a crown above his own hacked-in head.

I estimated I could be done in a week or two, though it actually took me almost two months to construct the whole room. I took photos of my work and texted them to the people I flirted with: my partner Avery; a girl from my MFA I had started dating; an ex living on the other side of the country. I knew I was building a monument of sorts, and I told myself it was for them. They'd heart each photo when it arrived. What I was making, I told myself, was inseparable from what I loved.

But as I worked, the fear didn't dissipate, it only mutated and evolved. Soon, the miniature began entering my dreams, too: My feet were doll's feet, squishing out paint as they walked. My drawers filled with red. I started carrying the model out of my bedroom at night to keep myself safe from its psychic energy, but the dreams didn't stop.

One evening, I planned to spend a few hours gluing the walls of the model together but, when I sat down, I burst into tears. I had been looking at Andrew's hatcheted face, even though I had seen it for many days already: a clay application I modeled to one-tenth scale, too, painted and scored in shades of red and deep purple with brushes the size of an eyelash. The purple was the same color of my father's skin when he was drinking. It had been just over four years since he'd died. I called Avery, who picked up on the third ring.

"I can't do this anymore," I said. "But I feel like I have to." I was halfway through the model, and the only way out seemed to be through. By continuing to work, I felt, I could free myself from two ghosts: my father's and Lizzie's.

"You're such a baby," they said, as I started to cry.

I used X-ACTO knives and an old boxcutter to build the dollhouse, slicing plywood into quarter-inch strips for the boards. I cut whole sheets of plyboard into the frame of the house, wallpapering the doorframes one by one. In the whittling, sawing, sanding, and staining that I needed to make each warped floorboard, I got lost, and because I was lost, I assumed the quiet parts of me were healing how they needed to. The dollhouse was the problem, or rather the solution, I told myself. The book was the problem—not my father's death, not me.

But as I built, I remembered him all over again anyway. My father wrote poetry, like I did—the first person to teach me to write. He loved to sit in our backyard, drinking his tumblers full of boxed Franzia and watching birds. He named me after his grandfather, a Polish name that was Anglicized into his own—so really, he named me after himself. He talked about me in extremes—deep pride or disappointment, but never anything in between. He loved to sing but wasn't very good at it. He only beat me once.

The thing was, as I cut the floorboards of the miniature, I was also cutting myself to shreds, using the same X-ACTO knives I did for the model. I'd text a lover, pour myself a shot, and only after I was done I'd cry. At the time, it felt like the only way through, like I wasn't hurting myself at all but rather committing myself to a new project.

When my father first hit me, it was several years after I saw the play about Lizzie. I was eleven. I had stayed out late and missed dinner, and he backed me into a corner and kept hitting until he didn't. It almost felt like I deserved it. How could I not think of the punishments that had been doled out to me and the ones I yearned to dole out myself? How could I not think of Lizzie, too?

"He loved you," my mother said frequently. "Despite his flaws, he was filled with love."

The year my father was hospitalized, he wrote me an email. I opened it on my phone in the corner of a dance floor on New Year's Day at 3 a.m., and read, between thuds of bass and bodies whirling: *You are not my daughter. Because you grew up with a sister who had died before you, because we did not hide it from you, that is why you're fucking up your body.* My father said: *Your mother's inability to conceal her grief is why your gender and sexuality is wrong.*

At that moment, watching my boyfriend dancing in the center of the room, I decided not to talk to my father ever again. In fact, I wished him dead. For five months, I didn't talk to him, even as my mother encouraged me to reach out again. It was only an impulse, nagging and inarticulatable, that led to me responding to his fourth apology, meeting for coffee, and setting the terms of our relationship moving forward. A week later he'd enter the hospital, and by the end of the summer, like I'd wished, he would be gone.

"I *know* you love me," I said in my email back to him, agreeing to meet, "but please stop hurting me."

My first book was not an act of forgiving my father, but, as linked as it was to his death, I dedicated it to him anyway. I wrote the book as a hidden autobiography, a way to think about how queerness and violence—verbal and physical and sexual—are often inextricable. I wrote it content in the knowledge that if anyone tried to read me into the work, they'd have to do the labor of reading past the innumerable differences between Lizzie's life and my own: our geographies, our class statuses, our genders. But I dedicated it to my father—including his birth and death dates on the first page like a tombstone—because I hoped some readers would try to name a shared hurt between me and her that I still couldn't even name myself. The idea of understanding him terrified me. And later, I started the dollhouse, without even consciously realizing it, right after his birthday. The book was intertwined with him, so, of course, the miniature was, too.

I didn't imagine murdering my father, like I believe Lizzie had, but I did dream him dead. Then it was actually happening and all I could feel was guilt. My father's slow death in the hospital was terrible, not at all what I was dreaming—but I had been dreaming it. Writing isn't healing, but I understand why I thought it could be; the book felt like the only foothold I had for my grief and guilt. Who, in our country, could see that synchronicity in death and not think the only way out was through work?

Cutting anything down can be a way to stay alive, but it can also distract from the other work of living as well. This was what my dreams tried to tell me; this was the same mistake I made while starting the dollhouse, too. A life slivering bits away isn't a life at all: In the aftermath of making the model, I'd feel alive and ashamed and above all still in pain, hiding in long-sleeve shirts and oversize pants splattered with the paint I covered the dollhouse in. It wasn't purifying; it wasn't redeeming; it just continued.

But even despite this, even if hurting myself didn't help, the dollhouse did. Paradoxically, through its endless rehearsals, through my prolonged return to Lizzie Borden's life, I eventually felt less haunted. It empowered me, and when I needed to stop working on it, I took a break—from the project, from hurting myself. I wonder if Frances

Glessner Lee, as much as I hate her work, felt the same relief in working and relief in stopping, too. In breaking my grief open to make my book, and then breaking myself open to make my model, I told myself I was doing the work—hurtling toward an endpoint I felt I deserved. I told myself I was free.

So of course I took space from the dollhouse. During my time off, I journaled, drank kava, saw my lovers, and texted my ex. I cried when I could. Over several weeks, I tried to stop working in miniature, living as largely as I could. I wrote and I laughed, and in exchange the dreams subdued. I held space for the complexity of the grief in its totality. I healed myself through the work, and then I stopped. I stopped.

But really, that last part was a lie. I stopped making the dollhouse, but I didn't stop anything else. I kept cutting until I was broken once again. And as I kept going (in actuality), the nightmares didn't cease; they kept getting worse until eventually I ceased dreaming anything at all. Like the twist at the end of a horror film, I thought by working I was setting myself free, but some other deep clawing hunger got released in me instead. The horror I had been trying to escape was inside me all along.

Lizzie Borden, the story goes, loved her father. Or at least, she said that she loved her father, often and publicly, before and after the murder. There are pieces of evidence toward a reciprocal love: Lizzie gave him a ring as a present when she was still a teenager, and he wore it on his finger until he died. I loved my father, too. But love and hurt do not exist especially far away from each other; and to admit one is not to deny the existence of the other. Andrew Borden, witnesses and newspapers said, was stingy; he was punishing; he was cruel. My father, too, loved me; and he, too, was stingy and punishing and cruel. This is what stood out so much to me about Lizzie's life as well: Her hurt was smartly concealed—to acknowledge harm would be to create a motive; how (if we extend this thought) the violence she caused was itself caused by something she refused to name. The love, and the hurt, are linked.

Of course, I'm speculating, but it's a speculation many people have shared over the years. The psychiatrist Jean Kim makes this point in a 2016 *Rolling Stone* article written by Elizabeth Yuko about the case: The Borden murders, she states, "reflect . . . the reality of violence in private families, even ones that seem outwardly affluent or normal." The murders were so violent, the thinking goes, there had to have been a deeper cause. Lizzie chopped her father's face apart, splitting an eyeball. You don't do that if you're not motivated by *something*. If there's not some cause for rage, merited or not, you don't act that way toward either of your guardians—for she killed her stepmother in an equally violent way, attacking her from the back and collapsing her skull.

I realize this is a slippery slope, justifying the violence Andrew and Abby Borden received by speculating about unconfirmed misdeeds. I realize I risk adhering to an inverted version of the same ideas of punishment Frances Glessner Lee adhered to—that the guilty need to receive justice and that Lizzie was the instrument of that. I'm ignoring the possibility that if or when Lizzie killed, she was afraid of what she was doing, too; I'm smoothing over her own legacy, much as others did when she was demonized for decades or more recently hailed as a pop-culture image of feminist retribution. ("Men don't have to know things, Bridget," Lizzie Borden says with a trembling, brave tone to her lover in the 2018 Chloë Sevigny–Kristen Stewart biopic made about her life. "Women do.") So instead of speculating more, I'll talk about my own fears, not hers.

I was afraid when I made the model of Andrew Borden's murder. I was afraid I had willed my father to die, and I was afraid that he would never stop haunting me after his death, and above all I was afraid I would keep hurting myself until I was all used up. I thought by building the model of another life that scared me, I could convert these fears into something physical and make them more manageable in turn. I thought this labor meant my complicated relationship with my father would remain buried instead of resurfacing, exorcising my own trauma neatly in a corner of a room. By making the model, I thought, I wouldn't have to ever verbalize what happened, what my father said to me or how he acted or how I acted in turn; and much like my earlier book, our relationship would be concealed between the lines. I thought that if I cut in miniature, that in the macro—where I led my life—I would be safe. And, just like Lizzie, my guilt would be acquitted.

When my father and I met up after his email, he was apologetic. He was slow in his movements. And he was drunk. "Forgive me," he said. Where we met, the buds on the trees—cherry blossoms—were white, and they were red, like they had been splattered with blood. We hugged goodbye awkwardly, and when he lurched away from me to return to the hotel room, the only thought I had was how small he looked, how alone. Afterward, I went to grab a drink with my mother, and together, over hibiscus cocktails, we talked about our complicated relationship with the man who shaped me so much. "He hurt you," she said again, "but he cares."

Frances Glessner Lee's miniatures stuck with me because they attempted to make order out of fear. But really, all they did was simplify a life into its most violent moments. They tell a viewer to look at the dead body and see every accumulated object—sewing machine or delicate house slippers—as accessories to a murder. When I was building my model, I bought a doll-size full-length mirror off eBay, placed at the front of the room, closest to anyone seeing it, but no one has commented on that. The only reason they would, I suspect, is if the mirror itself were cracked or marred—a broken clue as opposed to a detail from the clutter of a life. Friends who see the dollhouse instead look at the violent parts, which were, after all, the ones I spent the most time on: the head of Lizzie's father or the cracks in the floorboards, painted a crimson seeping red just like in my dream. I don't blame them. When I looked at Lee's miniatures, I did the same thing: I zeroed in on the violence and ignored everything else. When I dreamed, I only dreamed of things that hurt. When I woke, I worked until I couldn't, and then cut myself again.

After I finished the model, I moved it into my spare room so I wouldn't stare at it anymore. Then, I checked myself into the psych ward; and then I wrote these words. Now, every morning I see it in the living room when I sit with my coffee, legs still bearing the marks I made making my model. This, I think, was what scared me about Lizzie Borden's life. Once you slice into something, you can never take it back. Once you make a mark, it's on you forever. The blood that I dripped onto the model settled into the floorboards, mixing with the crimson paint, just like I knew it would all along. The father I made in miniature was as dead as my own, and all I had left was grief.

What is loss if not another kind of tumbling out of control? What is a wound if not the measure of life? Everyone I love has been hurt again and again, and each time they've emerged; everyone I love has lost themselves in so many dreams, but most have awakened. I'm sure my father—whose own father died when he was a teenager—was no different, even if he hurt me anyway. In the other room, the doll father's porcelain face glistens with gore, fresh as a memory, christened bright as a setting sun. *You can always stop*, it seems to say; *you can always start again*. What did he dream of? What were his own regrets, the violences he endured, too? What marks did he make on himself over his own hate- and love-filled life?

"I love you," my father had told me over the phone two days before he died, speaking slurred and slow through his stroke. "I can't wait to see you soon."

III.

We keep the wolves outside by living well.

—**ANGELA CARTER,** ***THE BLOODY CHAMBER***

Preliminary Materials for a Theory of the Werewolf Girl

1.

Halloween 2003. I am nine years old and have graduated to making my own costumes. On my chin, a ragged dark brown beard stretches out, barely attached with spirit gum; my hair, hastily dyed, almost matches it. In the picture, I'm wearing a heavy tan denim coat that doesn't quite fit—I was growing so fast then we bought all my clothes a size up to increase their longevity. I'm biting my upper lip with my canines. And in thick eyeliner I colored my nose black, drew a mottled snout below. I was nine, and werewolves were my favorite thing.

Who wouldn't be obsessed with werewolves at that age, in that body? It was the changing of it that was so exciting: The chance to shed my skin for something new and silky underneath, to grow until I was soft all over, not just on top of my head. For werewolves, change was violent and frightening, but so was my future puberty. And unlike my puberty—which I feared would be hard and harsh, jutting out angles and deepening crevices—there was a softness allowed in the werewolf's transformation. In movies, in books, stalking and swishing through the woods on their heels, claws extended, they moved with a grace deeply familiar to me: a feminized grace, almost delicate. Like the adults in my life I loved and respected, werewolves asserted their own kind of beauty. Werewolves avoided the trap of the masculine and the feminine, I thought; they just were. And by being one, perhaps I could, too.

At nine, I was a wisp of a child, with hair I wore long even then, and whenever I'd walk down the street with my mom, strangers would stop us with smiles on their faces, telling her: "What a beautiful daughter you have! She looks just like you!" She ignored them, and while I viewed these moments with irritation at the time, secretly something inside me felt thrilled: a moment of recognition. Look, I thought. Change. In my sleep, after all, I dreamed of transformations, too: breasts popping out of my shirt, hair growing thick between my legs until my genitals were completely obscured. A woman, says that famous '90s new-age book, *is* a wolf. I was just picking up what they had left behind.

My favorite movie at that time was *The Wolf Man*, the 1941 film that Universal Studios commissioned when their other monsters stopped making money and they needed new blood. The film, draped in fog and evil Roma, was about a man, Lawrence Talbot, who goes to visit his father in Wales. Talbot is a giant of a man, but a soft one; he doesn't know how to talk to women and has a face surprisingly gentle for his size, all dark blinking eyes and slightly parted lips. Throughout the movie Talbot struggles to get out from under his father's influence, and maybe this informed the casting: The actor who played Talbot, Lon Chaney Jr., was the son of the most famous horror actor of the silent era. Watching the movie, it's no wonder I empathized with him: He goes from being a soft man to a softer other thing. After the transformation, his nails, meant to resemble a wild animal's, look lacquered in the studio lighting. His heels raise, walking more delicately on his toes as if wearing stilettos. And in close-ups, Talbot's eyes, long-lashed and soft, look like a woman's eyes, bubbling over with a quiet sadness at what his body had become.

In almost every werewolf movie, no one wants to be a werewolf. The transformation is one that appears to exaggerate masculine features, or their stereotypes—body hair, muscle, a roar of a voice. *Were*, after all, is Old English for "man," not "woman." In transforming into a wolf, what we associate with men is emphasized. But that's not the same thing as becoming a man. Most people, after all, can't tell male or female wolves apart.

In werewolves, I see a refusal to become what others want of you despite whatever pressure you might feel—and in the wildness of their transformation I saw a future, too. Hair may sprout, voices may crack and deepen; so yes, werewolves' transformations are a kind of puberty, both freeing and monstrous. (The transformation itself, linked monthly to the moon and lasting several days at a time, becomes a ritualized bloodletting, almost menses.) But they refuse schemas of the expected; fundamentally, werewolves still transform in surprising ways. And my own puberties—both of them—were freeing and monstrous in turn.

I realize there's a danger in this identification, regardless of which way you cut it: If werewolves are linked to puberty, then they reinscribe the idea of biological puberty as destiny. On the other hand, if werewolves are linked to a second embodied change, one that happens after first puberty—in other words, if werewolves, as I see them, are trans—they align a little too neatly with the idea of trans people, and women in particular, as violent predators.

But regardless of how much I want to trouble this concept, it still doesn't change the force of that identification with werewolves as a child. It still doesn't change the way that, through my whole life, they've shaped how I've understood change. It doesn't change the second tattoo I ever got, which takes up my full right thigh—a woodcut from the 1500s of a werewolf wearing what looks suspiciously like a gaff, standing in splendor and horror alike. It doesn't change the love I feel for them, even as I know how that love might be weaponized.

The feminist fantasy and horror writer Angela Carter writes brilliantly about changing in her story "The Werewolf," from her 1979 collection *The Bloody Chamber*. In the story, an inversion of "Little

Red Riding Hood," a girl goes to visit her grandmother, but en route is accosted by a wolf. Reacting quickly, the girl cuts the wolf's right paw off and the wolf whimpers away ("wolves," Carter writes, "are less brave than they seem"). The girl pockets the paw in her picnic basket and heads to her grandmother's house, but grandmother is sick now, skin blistering with heat. When the girl goes to unpack the oatcakes she was tasked with bringing, the wolf's paw tumbles out, but now it's a hand, old and freckled and still wearing the grandmother's wedding band. She calls the neighbors, and they chase the woman, clutching her bloody stump, out into the snow and stone her to death. "Now the child lived in her grandmother's house," Carter's story ends; "she prospered."

We know nothing of the grandmother's desires, whether becoming a wolf was a curse or an escape for her. But after being found out as a wolf she is punished, her bodily transformation a sin only treatable by death. And by exposing her grandmother's secret perversion the granddaughter triumphs, changing her own life dramatically for the better by killing her grandmother. The grandmother passes as normal, but it's a precarious passing, and once her secret's uncovered, she's killed. The capacity to change, Carter suggests, is swiftly punished by society. The werewolf, she says, can never triumph. The villagers will always be incensed by the sheer fact of being tricked. How scary, Carter's story implies, to not know you're even looking at a body like mine.

But maybe I'm looking at this wrong. Things that aren't a choice aren't always a burden. Who hasn't wanted to be stripped of agency but in, like, a hot way? Who hasn't wanted to slide sure as a moon ascends in the skies towards something not you, something beautiful instead? Who hasn't dreamed of a life beyond the moment of change, too?

When I had my first dream of turning into a woman, I was six or seven. I felt horrified. I didn't even write the dream into my dream journal, which I kept religiously. Instead, I prayed about it. But over the next ten years, I had more dreams of the same transformation: I entered a haunted house and looked in a mirror to see myself, all flowing gowns and sable hair; or I walked down the street and men started pursuing me with even greater wolfishness, until I looked down and saw a bosom gently swelling beneath my sweaty T-shirt; or I became a cartoon character, a popular one, and in the blink of an eye grew hips and eyelash extensions and pouty lips.

When these dreams started, I was still prepubescent. It would be easy to think of them as being about that first puberty going wrong, but puberty didn't come until I was seventeen, and when it did come, it was anticlimactic to the point of nonexistence. I shot up a foot, and my voice dropped to a throaty whisper, but nothing else changed. My hair, limited to my armpits and right above my pubic mound, was sparse and so blond you could barely see it. Shaving my face was a formality at best and my eyelashes were long, lips full. People still viewed me as a girl. I had changed, but only the sort of change that reveals what you will eventually become: a moon poking awkwardly out from behind a cloud, skin molting into fur and that molting back into skin again. I felt almost disappointed. I had begun a process of transformation but knew, even then, that it was incomplete.

But I'm familiar with the thrall of incompletion. In the first draft of this essay, before I arrived at the precarious equation of werewolves and trans people, I argued for a more basic claim, one perhaps indefensible: that werewolves are women. Werewolves, the argument went, were soft and women were soft; they both needed to defend themselves against a prejudiced world. I asserted this because I love werewolves and see myself in werewolves and I myself am a woman. But of course, werewolves aren't women; werewolves are werewolves. Besides, it wasn't womanhood at all, but the potential that connected me to werewolves in the first place—the means to change I wanted all along. And as much as that desire toward change is framed as predatory, is framed as damaging, is framed as monstrous, I still feel it to this day. It's my own full moon. I have to continue to assert it, because it's part of what keeps me, and those like me, alive.

One more film. In the 2000 movie *Ginger Snaps*, being a werewolf and going through puberty *are* both intense changes, and ones that are linked. In the film, Ginger Fitzgerald, a moody and goth teenager who hasn't had her first period yet, is bitten by a werewolf. Immediately she begins bleeding from both her wounds and between her legs; the wounds heal overnight; fibrous hairs start emerging from the wounds and then everywhere across Ginger's body. Slowly, over the course of a whole month, Ginger grows more and more lupine until by the film's conclusion she's all wolf, slavering across the unfinished basement where she and her sister sleep.

Ginger Snaps is loosely told from Ginger's sister's perspective. Bridget, a year younger, hides her body, draping it in heavy flannels and goth-'90s fashion. As Ginger starts to flaunt her growing curves—for after the bite Ginger's body becomes more womanly before it becomes less—Bridget grows increasingly upset with her sister. "I thought we were the same!" she screams. But Ginger hates her body, too, or at least does before she goes full wolf. As hair blooms everywhere across her body, she's devastated, trying to shave it all off with a pink Bic and leaving bloody streaks up and down her arms in the process. "I'm not supposed to have a hairy chest!" she cries to Bridget after she starts to change. "That's *fucked*!"

When I started hormones, my eyes softened, and my nose shrank. My lips puffed out slightly more. And my body hair, already scant, started to disappear completely: Armpits thinned out to twin patches of fuzz. Pubic hair narrowed itself to a strip. The toothpick of hairs running up to my navel vanished. Several girls I knew had to engage in long, painful electrolysis sessions over their whole bodies, so I was grateful that it was one more expensive and painful procedure avoided, but I felt conflicted about it all, like another part of me was being erased, too. I grew up around hairy women, adopted and raised by forest-legged dykes from early college on. Losing my own hair felt like losing a connection to them, too.

Late in the film, Ginger walks through a party on Halloween, hirsute breasts hanging out of her plunging neckline, and everyone runs away screaming or wants to fuck her. (Werewolves, the movie suggests, have chasers, too.) Unlike in other werewolf movies, the changes Ginger goes through seem permanent, marking her indelibly into the future. She grows a tail that she tucks underneath her pants like a dick. Her voice thickens into a growl. But because she looks more wild than the other girls, she's more desired. Eventually Ginger dies, because if you look different, it's hard to stay alive for long—but not before she kills, and kills, and kills.

There are other ways to read Ginger's transformation: As someone born, nominally, with the "body of a woman," a body that grows furred and lithe, she changes inside a framework of transmasculinity as much as one of femininity. I don't want to discount the validity of that reading, any more than I want to negate the experiences of any of my trans siblings. But I watched the film shortly after I had started hormones myself, and as she prowled down the halls, abject and beautiful, I saw someone scared of the change and then growing to love it. My body started to grow hair, too, and then it stopped, transforming into its own well of strength. Regardless of what direction Ginger was moving in, I saw a kind of sisterhood. The beauty of werewolves—despite their problems—is that all they do is change, and that *is* trans. In Ginger, I saw someone like me.

2.

The whole transsexual thing: Sometimes people can tell you're ripening to the point of change and instead of ushering you forward, take a bite out of you instead. Sometimes they take a bite after you've ripened, too.

In 2018, I was going to an issue launch for a social justice–themed arts magazine I worked for. I pulled on some old jeans that made my ass look really good, a tank top, and my favorite jacket, oxblood leather sitting tight against my tits. I had to transfer trains, so I got off at Lafayette and walked a block, shivering slightly in the January cold. When I got back to the platform, I started to perspire, unzipped my leather jacket. My breasts bounced slightly as I did so.

Then I looked over. I was waiting near the underside of a staircase where a man in dirty-looking clothes sat, staring at me. There was a hunger in his eyes, and he smiled when I made eye contact. His penis dangled out of his pants, and his right hand was moving up and down, faster and faster. Then he made a quiet yip and ejaculate splashed out of him and onto my shoe. I could still feel it through the canvas with my little toe once I got onto the train; it was milky and warm.

When I got to the issue launch, I was not myself. My hair was frazzled. My affect was uneven. I smiled too wide, but not in my eyes. In the photos of the event, I look unhinged, barely present. All the while I was waiting, counting down the seconds for it to be over.

I couldn't afford a cab, so once the event ended, I took the train back home again. My heart skipped a beat once I was at Lafayette, but the man seemed to be gone. So I transferred back onto the C train and rattled back to my home, the crumbling Victorian that I lived in with twenty roommates.

Once I was back home, I called the transit authority hotline to tell them what happened. "I'm sorry to hear that ma'am," said the person on the other line. "I'd be happy to put you in touch with the police to file an incident report."

"I don't want to be in touch with the police," I said. "I just want you to know that there's a man at the train station masturbating at women. Can't you just keep an eye out?"

"We'll transfer you over to the police, ma'am," they said.

I hung up, but for days afterwards, I received calls from unknown numbers. When I didn't pick up, I'd find new messages in my inbox. "Hello, miss," they'd say. "This is the NYPD. We're calling in response to the subway incident you reported. If you don't give us information, you can be held in contempt, and we can take action against you, too." After a few weeks, the calls eventually stopped. I don't know what happened to the man.

He wasn't a werewolf, but he bit me. I wasn't a werewolf, either, but wished I could have been in my response, growled back at him or done anything else. Instead, at the moment of his contact, I started to remember every other bite taken out of my sweet flesh, all the other ways men had hurt me, too.

Change, of course, isn't only affirming. It's sometimes not even volitional, and werewolf stories reflect that, too. In the mainstream imagination, werewolves are frequently depicted as victims of their own hormonal appetites. They experience uncanny urges beyond the urge to transform. "His body a twitching tomb of unearthly desires!" breathlessly proclaims the copy on the original poster for *The Wolf Man*, reprinted on the back of the VHS tape I owned since I was a kid. Underneath the text, a painting of Lon Chaney Jr. hovering, claws extended, over an unconscious blond. Even how werewolves kill is an embodied experience—all ripping and mauling and splaying open. They seem to not have control over themselves at all.

That's the other danger in writing about werewolves as trans: To this day, narratives about trans people—and especially trans women—as uncontrollable groomers or violent rapists persist. (At the time of writing this, July 15, 2024, both political parties are united in their disdain of gender-affirming care for youth, and the second-highest grossing movie in the country is *Longlegs*, a horror film where Nicolas Cage plays a crypto-trans woman child abuser and murderer disrupting the nuclear family through his/her perversity. "It's so scary," say my cis friends. Ask me if I'm surprised.) At first glance, werewolves, who hurt others violently, can reflect those same paradigms. But I don't think raping someone and otherwise hurting them are the same. If your guts are ripped out, you feel it immediately, but for me, every time I've been violated, it's taken years to fully realize the magnitude of what's happened. Werewolves are messy, but not in a sexual way—despite the "desires" that *The Wolf Man*'s poster art invoked. Rather, a werewolf just splays a body for the sake of it, making a meal of you. It's still a dangerous connection to risk, but one more discrete.

After the man came on me, I started experiencing flashbacks. A boy in high school blocking the door of his room as he jacked off mechanically at me. "I want to see the look in your eyes when I come," he said. Another boy who I trusted with my secrets touching me as I said no, stop. Years earlier in undergrad, when they first started to come back to me, I first called these instances rape. Regardless of legal definitions, they were violations, and they changed me. Then, I cried for weeks, stopped sleeping, had a mental breakdown, and entered therapy for the first time as an adult. But when the man in the subway stirred these feelings up again, I felt angry instead of endlessly sad, and in that way I knew I had started to change again. Even though the man was a stranger, not someone I trusted, he violated me, and that incensed me. *Oh yeah*, I thought, *this will just keep fucking happening*. I was in the middle of my MFA when he masturbated on me, and afterward I started writing poem after poem about wolves in response. I stapled together a loose-leaf booklet and brought it into workshop: *Wolf Inventory*, I called it. "What is wolf but wanting," I wrote. In wolves, I found a larger narrative of what was done to me, but I also saw what I could do in return.

I took the booklet I brought into workshop and sent it to a tiny online press, who loved it and then published it as a chapbook for free. Some people found and liked *Wolf Inventory*, but even those who enjoyed it didn't quite get what I was trying to say. "Wolves are predators," one review noted. "The book's brilliance is highlighting that." I wanted to say *yes, but*. The wolves in the book were sometimes men, but not always, and they certainly weren't always causing harm. More often than not, they were endangered, and scared. They refused victimhood and refused clean narratives of being aggressors. They refused a binary in general. They weren't werewolves, but also they kind of were. They were us.

The project was slightly incoherent, but through it, I started to draft out the ideas that still consume me to this day: questions of pain and transformation alike. True, in life, I see what is done in the name of desire, or power, or cruel want. These are things that shift us. But I also see the chance to transform, alter into things more powerful than we can believe. The were in werewolf doesn't just imply masculinity; it implies humanity, in all its capacity to hurt and hold alike. Unlike the pop culture cliché of the wolf, werewolves aren't driven solely by instinct. A part of them, the part from before the change, must remain. That's why werewolves matter to me—why they're so resonant to so many others, as well.

A few months after I published the chapbook, I received a small grant to make a film. I started making *Wolf Inventory: Movie Version* with Candace, a filmmaker also from the South. Together, we shot footage—hands digging through the dirt; the moon barely caught through a deep thicket of trees; me in a bright red dress and wolf face that we made ourselves from a nurse's surgical mask. Mainly, though, we talked. "Every boy who hurt me," I mused to her as we shared cigarettes outside, "I thought I could trust." V, who fingerpicked along to King Crimson albums in his dorm room and said he masturbated at me to teach me a lesson. B, who I told all my secrets to and would hold me even though I said no and unbuttoned my pants and slid his hand in and I said no to that, too, and he kept moving his hand between my legs as if I invited him to. Jimmy in kindergarten, who I don't know what happened with, but something did because I still haven't stopped dreaming of him and waking up in panic even now. They were my friends. And because of that I let them in, and they took things from me.

The film we were making was designed as a recuperation of these violences, a way to respond with a violence of our own. "Men," we said in late-night conversations over tumblers full of bourbon, "behaved in wolfish ways toward us." So we would become werewolves in return. We shot footage: Me running in the woods, watched through the cameras. Me eating pasta primavera for dinner, shot through the window and splattered with red. Candace and I stalking down a dim hallway wearing wolf masks and walking with deliberation. We filmed most of this at the residency I attended in late summer 2018 in rural Pennsylvania—a robber baron's home converted into a water research center. His house overflowed with things he had killed, and these things became a part of the movie, too: deer antlers woven together to make a mirror, falcons and wild turkeys taking stuffed flight above the fireplace.

Gradually, we pieced together the parts of a short film as we were filming it, leaving the general structure intentionally sketchy. The grant wasn't much, but it was more money for an arts project than I had seen before, and we knew—especially because we were borrowing cameras and sound equipment from friends—that we could make it stretch out for several years. We finalized our plans at the end of the residency: We'd return there the following summer and finish the film, editing together a rough trailer from what we shot and using that to invite more collaborators to the project. But the following year I got accepted to a new series of writing retreats and Candace started a new job and got swamped with her MFA capstone, so we deferred it another year. Then the pandemic happened. By the end of 2021, we stitched together some of the footage we shot into a rough edit, uploaded it to an unpublished website alongside some introductory notes, and called the project finished. Rather than not living at all, we decided, the film would exist in fragments—a set of dangling threads rather than a full tapestry. Just like my memories of what happened to me, the film, too, lingered, a partial and incomplete record of violence bestowed and received.

The film failed in part because I'd been sidestepping the fact that werewolves hurt people after all. They don't transform into wolves for the sake of the transformation: They transform into them to kill. If there's a flaw in my methodology, a gaping hole where my theory should be, it's that. In *The Wolf Man*, Lawrence Talbot cries when he wakes up muddy and smeared in blood; in *Ginger Snaps*, Ginger pukes up a finger and weeps into the toilet bowl at what she's become. Fundamentally, werewolves are violent monsters, and that violence causes pain in themselves and their victims. But unlike brute animals, they remain human, with all the human feelings of guilt and grief that come with the killing. My metaphor, fundamentally, doesn't fit—or if it does fit still, it needs to acknowledge the harm we do to others, too.

When I myself started to change, it took me so long to reach any love toward what I was becoming, curdled or otherwise. In countless books and movies, werewolves fear the hair sprouting across their bodies, the changes they undergo. But look at their shimmer of fur, their long-lashed eyes, their lean athletic bounds across moonlit fields. Yes, werewolves kill; yes, werewolves maim; yes, werewolves create more of themselves every time they prowl. But is there something so wrong about more of us existing? Even if they hurt others, werewolves *are* still about moving from one body to another beautiful one—which is, after all, what I did after I learned I was trans in the first place. I learned to want in a more benign way. And in the wanting, I changed until, finally, I fell into community with others like me and felt at ease.

3.

Here's the trap I keep falling into again and again. I said they were boys, the ones who touched me and touched themselves looking at me, but that's not entirely true.

I had just finished my senior year of college when I found out. We were at a four-year high school reunion party in Durham, dozens of us crammed into the semi-finished basement of a classmate's parent's house. The house was easy to find: People whose faces looked almost familiar lingered outside. Everyone had undergone their own transformation since we graduated: eyebrows thinned and beards bloomed from formerly barren cheeks. Inside, pop music wobbled. A girl who I barely knew cornered me as soon as I entered, drunkenly wavering just several inches away from my face.

"It's soooooo brave that you've, you know. . . ." She trailed off, waving her hand up and down at my body. Someone had briefed her before I came. She paused thoughtfully. "We *knew* though, of course. You were living in the trans dorm, after all."

Someone else must have seen the look of confusion on my face, so they stepped in, too. "Didn't you hear? V and B started transitioning, too. You all were close, weren't you?"

The drunken girl squealed at this confirmation. "You were! You all should *totally* get drinks together . . . a girls' night! It would be so cute!"

I felt like moss was shot into my veins: Suddenly, everything felt damp and thick. "Excuse me," I said, and stumbled outside for air. I didn't even correct the two people deadnaming my assailants.

"If the werewolf is an inherently contradictory creature," writes Hannah Priest in the introduction to *She-wolf*, her anthology of critical essays on female werewolves, "so too is a woman." I just started to come into myself as a woman, and there they were as well: Taking up fucking space next to me when *they* had hurt *me*. I had built a whole narrative of my transition reclaiming control over my body from the ones who abused it first, and then it turned out they were just like me, too.

In naming this, it feels like I'm fashioning a weapon against myself—giving credence to the theories that wish to eliminate me and my kind. But if I transitioned because of the violences done to me, if those violences were done to me because I was femme, if I became myself more fully in response to the way that violence tried to strip me of that femininity—the fact that my assailants were also struggling with the same thing doesn't negate any of that reality. It is simpler to leave this story out, to unreveal it, but the truth is muddy and it complicates. The women who hurt me didn't do so because they were trans, and yet they are still trans and they did still hurt me. They are not my allies, and yet together we still linger in this uneasy space.

My father, after all, tried to masculinize me as well. I don't know what my dormmates' lives were like before they came to the school—but I know an incipient masculinity was draped over me like a hood, too. Hours in the garage with the punching bag. The set of weights in my bedroom that I would do bench presses on every night. Even running was an effort to change my body—to make it stronger, which is to say, in the dominant imagination, more like that of a man. I underwent my own transformations, and I rejected them, and I transformed again. People should be allowed to change for whatever reasons possible. It's in the changing that we get a chance to live.

It's not a werewolf story, but there's another instance of a woman transforming into a beast in Angela Carter's short story collection *The Bloody Chamber*. It's in her retelling of *Beauty and the Beast*, "The Tiger's Bride." The story starts off like the fairy tale: The girl, traded in a game of cards by her profligate father to a terrible beast, is held captive in a luxurious castle by clockwork servants as the beast, her captor, avoids her for days. But unlike in the fairy tale, the beast's only wish is to see the girl naked; do this, he proclaims in his booming beast voice, and then she will be returned to her father. The girl hesitates, and they dance around this for days until, finally pressured into acquiescence, she is taken to a remote river. There the beast shrugs off his liniments and the mask hiding his fur-covered features and stands nude and the girl does, too, and they look at each other briefly and then put their clothes back on.

But afterward the girl feels violated because, of course, she was, even if nothing else happened. So instead of going home to her father—who has grown rich from his trade—she wanders through the castle until she finds the beast again, pacing and fully an animal in his private chambers. And then, in the extraordinary end to the story, the beast begins to lick her, like a cat. As he licks, the girl tells us, "Each stroke of his tongue ripped off skin after successive skin, all the skins of a life in the world, and left behind a nascent patina of shiny hairs. My earrings turned back to water and trickled down my shoulders; I shrugged the drops off my beautiful fur." And the story ends.

There's a cruelty in me misrepresenting the girls who assaulted me as boys earlier in this essay, misgendering them and ascribing a masculinity they surely felt unsure in. But it would be a greater cruelty if I said who they were now, revealed their current names or identities. We don't talk. I don't want to ever see them. But they're still my sisters now. They should be allowed to live their lives, because regardless of our behavior so few of us are allowed that. I hope as their bodies changed, they got better, and never did what they did to me to anyone else. I hope they lay awake at night just as I do. I hope, I really do. Let me repeat it: I want them to live.

The Wolf Man ends when Lawrence Talbot is clubbed to death by his own father with a silver wolf's-head cane. As he dies, he turns back into a human, and his flesh is soft and full again. The film's mystical Roma character, an offensive stereotype if there ever was one, appears from the mist and gently presses his eyes closed. Then, closing her own eyes, she recites a poem, sending him into the afterlife. "The way you walked was thorny through no fault of your own," she says, "but as the rain enters the soil, the river enters the sea, so tears run to a predestined end.... Now you will find peace for eternity."

I thought of my childhood werewolves and my sisters and myself and fought back tears as I took another drag from my cigarette. The moon hung heavy and large in the sky above: a supermoon, charged with something far bigger than itself. I was charged, too, overflowed with spite. I had been changed and then I had changed myself again, and in many different ways, throughout a life that is breathlessly long, I will certainly continue to shift.

A former classmate, a tall lumbering boy who used to be a resident advisor on my hall, stumbled across the lawn and almost fell on me. "Sorry, man!" he yelled out behind his shoulder. Then he was gone, and it was just me and my thoughts of my assailants: Three women, alone in the dark. In the distance, something howled.

Devotion

1.

My sister was the first thing I believed in, even before God.

Chrissy died in a car crash almost two years to the day before I was born—my February 20 to her February 29, leap day. It was 3 a.m., and she was nineteen. She'd just discovered that the boy she was living with was cheating on her, so she drove the icy roads of Connecticut to chase him down. Her car hadn't been inspected recently, and the brakes failed when she hit a patch of ice. She swerved off the road and hit a tree. She died almost immediately.

"When she died," my mother told me, "I swore to myself I would become so good, I would be a saint."

Chrissy's things still hang on our wall—even now, thirty-three years later. Two faces, crying and laughing, made out of papier mâché; a jar of her baby teeth on a dresser. She was everywhere you looked, if you looked close. Her bright-green letter jacket from high school hung in my closet, and when I slipped it on it felt like she was holding me. She had a different father but the same mother so our features were similar, like me, but not: the same button nose and thick lips; different curlier, blond-brown hair. Her face is framed next to mine on top of the family piano, uncanny in our resemblance.

My mother got pregnant with Chrissy at fourteen, so her adult life was shaped almost exclusively by her presence. For my birth, I received a picture book that my mother drew and painted herself, depicting my sister sending me down from heaven to my parents laughing in joy. She was the reason I was conceived, I'd been taught—her sudden absence in my parents' life creating a void they then filled with me. My childhood was contoured by hers; growing up, stories about Chrissy floated ambiently through every conversation, waiting to settle down on a pair of lips and start being told:

- How she chased a group of catcallers down the street with a butcher knife and a dog on a chain

- How she found out one of her boyfriends was cheating on her and went over to his house, knocked on the door, and popped him straight in the face

- How as a teenager in Saint Thomas she had a knack for finding tarantulas, using sticks to nudge them out of holes in dirt and hold them up, wriggling, to the delight of the children nearby

Years later, my dad would send me the drunken email in which he accused me of transitioning because my mother was unable to grieve properly: My sister's absence flowed into me, made it impossible for me to live as a boy. At the time, I refused to think about Chrissy, pouring myself instead into Lizzie Borden, the father-killer.

My father was a devout Catholic, and after Chrissy's death became more so. Being raised in the shadow of Chrissy's ghost, he implied, caused me to replace the faith I was supposed to inherit from him with a needle through the flesh, a budding breast where piousness used to be. My mother raised me in a world, he insinuated, with a God who only took, and it was no wonder I turned away from him and Him alike.

"Your mother's a crazy bitch," he told me once, when he was drinking, "and she's trying to turn you against me."

My mother told the story of her trying to become a saint often, occasionally switching around the context in which it appeared but mainly using it to describe her own loss of faith. Chrissy had just died, so my mother committed herself to a life of service, hoping if her heart was pure enough, there was no way God wouldn't answer her prayers. She went to church as often as she could, attended daily Mass before driving to the small elementary school where she taught. She cooked meals for others. She prayed all the time. She tried to be an instrument, she said, of "perfect good," reflecting what the Church had taught her.

Now my mother's an atheist, but maybe her project was doomed to fail from the start. Right after Chrissy passed away, the Missionaries of Charity, nuns of the order of Mother Teresa, came to visit her and my father—part of their mission to comfort the afflicted. Wearing their blue-and-white habits, they filed into my parents' tiny house in Saint Thomas and sat down at the dining room table. My mother hurried in cups of tea and snacks on a little tray, eager for help.

But the nuns only engaged in small talk. They asked how life on the island was, what my parents spent their time doing. Neither of my parents were in any position to talk about any of this. Their daughter had just died. Almost everyone in their life was telling them, "God works in mysterious ways." They wanted guidance, and the nuns refused to give it. After a few minutes of conversation, the Missionaries of Charity cleared their throats and prepared to leave. "Pray and Jesus will alleviate your suffering," they told my parents. "Our daughter is fucking dead," my mother said. She kept going to Mass for a decade afterward, but this, I suspect, began her long disillusionment with the Church. As they left, the nuns didn't even clear their plates.

A few years ago, I visited my mother in Richmond, and on my request, she brought down the big box from the attic, my sister's things that weren't on display. We pawed through handler's permits from her time in food service, expired club ID cards to Barnacle Bill's, the bar on the waterfront. And we looked through dozens of letters and cards sent to my mother in the months following her daughter's death. Over a third of them alluded to "God's plan," said my mother's suffering would be over soon.

After the nuns' visit, my mother realized, nothing seemed to be changing. As good as she tried to be, her prayers went unaddressed. My sister's ghost remained in the house, acknowledged by my mom but not my dad, who was only her stepfather, after all—even if he had been in Chrissy's life for over a decade himself. As for me, I had pieces of her life but never the complete *her*, instead peering at an earlier family life less touched by grief or more touched by God.

As we pawed through driver's licenses and graduation photos, I asked my mother what she prayed for. It wasn't an end to her pain, as I or the countless well-wishers had assumed. She wished for just one thing, day after day, night after night: That her daughter wasn't afraid when she died.

My ex-girlfriend Siobhan was also ex-Catholic. I started falling back in love with her early in the pandemic. We called each other on the phone with increasing frequency: once a month, then twice, then almost once a week. At first, they were spur-of-the-moment conversations, but soon we began to plan them, scheduling dates over text message and inscribing them in our iCals. We'd talk for hours.

I was still living in the collective house in Brooklyn then, a four-story Victorian with long mahogany staircases. Out of COVID fear, I mainly shut myself in my room, barely talking to my roommates. This was April 2020 and uncertainty was in the air. I, with my own disabilities and an immunocompromised partner, feared any connection that wasn't virtual. Hence: Siobhan, who I had dated two years ago and never *really* broke up with when she left for Portland to finish school.

Separated by thousands of miles, we spent most of our second relationship together watching movies over Zoom. We watched *Dogtooth* and I covered my eyes when a young girl pulled out her canine teeth to escape the cult she was raised in; we watched *Melancholia* and winced as Kirsten Dunst, nude and deeply depressed, struggled to get into a bathtub. Our informal series ended when we watched *Audition*, a film about a woman who tortures a man who tried to groom her by plunging needles deep into his skin and garroting wire around his ankle. The movies were meant to bring us closer—an endurance contest of forced intimacy. As the credits rolled, Siobhan ran offscreen to throw up. Feeling bad, we realized, didn't have value in and of itself; it only made us feel bad.

But before we came to this realization and stopped entirely, we watched *Saint Maud*, which ended up being the movie that stuck with us the most. Rose Glass's film, released in 2019, was about Catholicism—or at least a torturous sort of Christianity—and one woman's increasingly dysfunctional relationship to her faith. Maud lives in England, devout to the point of restriction. She is a caretaker for an older lesbian, a former dancer. Maud clearly longs for this woman, but rechannels her longing toward a desire to save her soul.

Maud tortures herself throughout the film, and I felt a reluctant kinship with her through my own practice of self-harm. Up until that point, any crisis I experienced was an excuse to enact punishment in response: skipping meals, running mile after mile until I got shin splints, and, in my shared dorm in high school, staying up late past when anyone else would be awake and punching myself until my gut purpled. I connected to the movie because Maud, too, found salvation through suffering: Throughout the whole film, whenever she hears God speak to her, she punishes herself afterward. In the movie's second most intense scene, Maud picks up a man at a bar for quick, empty sex. As she rides him, she sees her hands collapsing his sternum open, fisting the purpled organs beneath. After sex, she hears the voice of God again emanating from a cockroach in her living room, and then she floats off the floor and bends completely in half. She shoves thumbtacks in her feet. She burns herself on a stove. Each moment purifies the pain she feels more ambiently through the rest of her life.

Siobhan and I wisecracked while we watched these movies together, typing bon mots over the Zoom chat. It was surreal getting closer to her while we lived so far away, and the intimacy we shared watching these films was only partial; we couldn't even hold hands. But that ghost intimacy drew us closer, too: The barrier of the screen and the distance between us meant that when we were together on our Zoom calls, we were paying total attention to each other. When we watched *Saint Maud*, we were quiet until the credits rolled, as if we had seen something transformational. "I loved that," Siobhan said to me when it was done, and then we showed the film to everyone we knew.

Saint Maud was scary because it made sense: Its protagonist was traumatized and Catholic and insane, and we were, too. Where most films would tokenize that insanity by making Maud a background figure to another character's more palatable spiritual journey, the director refuses this trope. Maud's own subjectivity is centered up until the second-to-last shot of the film. Until the film's end, her reality is the only one we see.

At the climax of the movie, Maud goes to the dancer's house. She had lost her caretaking job several days earlier, when she slapped the dancer after she mocked Maud's faith. In the days following, Maud, still uncomfortable admitting her own attraction to her employer, becomes even more obsessed with saving her soul. (Devotion to the Lord, as the nuns who visited my mother demonstrated, inspires cruelty, too.) At the dancer's house, she makes a tentative advance and is rebuffed. In response, hallucinating her employer as a demonic temptress, she stabs a pair of kitchen shears into her object of desire's neck and then self-immolates with a jug full of acetone in front of a sea of people on the rocky beachfront.

At first, when Maud burns at the end, it seems like she's finally entering God's grace, wings sprouting from her back golden and gossamer-thin. Then, we cut to her ablaze, panic stirring in her eyes, as the truth of her actions finally seizes her. Maud's reversion to Christianity, in initial response to her own guilt over someone's death, only led to further death; her own insistence on self-punishment, denying her feelings for the dancer, didn't purify her at all.

After Chrissy's death, my mother and I both clung to faith—my mother to Catholicism, and me to Chrissy herself. We both thought we could burn away the parts of us that weren't devoted to things greater than ourselves, replace one type of pain with another. We were both shadowed by death, but on different sides. So was Maud—a shadow that led to her own suppression of her desires, her own punishment. I watched the movie with someone I longed for and also couldn't reach, separated by the wide gulf of the country between us. I punished myself, too.

After the movie ended, Siobhan signed off the Zoom window, and then I was alone. I closed my laptop, sat back in my bed, and thought of Maud. Nothing in her life had changed from the path her initial devotion led her down—no grace, no sainthood, no redemption. Just like my mother had dreaded with Chrissy, at that moment of Maud's death, the only thing present was fear.

2.

As far back as I can remember, when I got too scared, I'd dissect my features in the mirror—eyes lidded, jaw slack, clinical in my ability to float above the body into a place of observation alone. I wanted to access this clarity and disembodiment at the same time on my own terms, be able to dissect and peel away the ridges of my brain like I did my face and body. I didn't even realize I was longing to dissociate more freely, or the extent to which I could already drift away from myself. I just wanted to clean the slate more fully. As I stared into the glass, my features would blur: slivered off in my memory until they became feminized and blurry, like the paintings of the saints that lined the church library where we had Sunday school.

Driven by this desire to be both in my body and not, in fifth grade I tried to teach myself hypnosis. Crouched under the oak tree at the corner of the playground, I read the turtleback how-to guide I got from the public library, twists of grass tickling my ankles as I practiced through the pages. I wiggled my finger in front of the eyes of boys who'd asked me to. "Do you feel anything?" I'd ask, and they, disappointed, would respond that they felt nothing at all.

This precipitated a larger pattern of disappointment, both with my new hobby and with myself. I tried to hypnotize myself, whispering tidings of goodness and locking eyes with myself in the mirror, but nothing happened. I tried to hypnotize peers from the playground outside, but still nothing happened. When men would follow me on bicycles weaving menacingly through the streets, I imagined driving them away with the power of my incredible new abilities. Once, I whispered, "You're getting sleepy" to a man who had been following me for blocks, and he smiled a thick-toothed smile. "I know," he said, and I started to run.

I don't know if my sister dissociated, too, but in photos of her, she sometimes looks away from the camera, refusing to meet a gaze, and it seems she's lost in thought about something. In my favorite snapshot of her, she extends an arm behind her head, the muscles in her neck and bicep tense and thick. But her head angles away; it's as if she simultaneously posed and didn't know a picture was being taken at all. Lost in rumination, her eyelashes taper downward and lips pucker slightly, and she looks beautiful and fierce and unknowable at the same time. She looks like me.

Hypnosis was a faith-based practice for me, in that I had faith it would work. How could I not, when I achieved my own less intense version of it staring in my bedroom mirror each night? My whole life up to that point I dealt with my issues by concentrating on them without direction, feeling but not doing. Why wouldn't I think that hypnosis, which started with close attention, would be a skill easily within my reach?

Faith, like desire, is rarely on your own terms: If you can only sometimes choose what you have faith in, you can never select what has faith in you. Hypnosis, distant as a sister, was there briefly and then disappeared. Just like my mother's own stint with her faith, I gave it up, lasting six weeks before I stopped entirely. As much as I wanted to, I simply didn't believe in the practice enough to stay. It shadowed me while I was lucky enough to hold it, and then, quick as Maud's own consumption in flames at the end of the film, it was gone.

The mid-twentieth century thinker, revolutionary, and Jewish-turned-Catholic mystic Simone Weil writes of her own urges to disappear, to lose herself in the thick recesses of the mind. She refused to feel anything but the body and its own pain, and I read her during the miserable January I spent in the psych ward. There, I underlined half of the sentences in my book, a slim Routledge academic edition with a floating red balloon, like in *It*, on the cover. I wondered if my sister, who briefly considered entering the Church, would feel the same relation: how you can manage pain by paying closer attention to it. Weil writes:

> At a certain moment, pain is lessened by projecting it into the universe, but the universe is impaired; the pain is more intense when it comes home again, but something in me does not suffer and remains in contact with a universe which is not impaired.... Attention, taken to its highest degree, is the same thing as prayer. It presupposes faith and love.

Maybe it's no wonder that Weil thought attention to pain was a way to access the divine. She grew up rich, taught to ask for things from an early age. She tried to help others in return, volunteering for countless freedom struggles, but a mix of clumsiness and the incompetence at hard work fostered by a childhood of no work at all limited what she could do. She worked as a farmer and as a factory worker, but barely lasted several weeks at each job. When the Spanish Civil War began, Weil immediately volunteered as a cook for the anarchists but got recused two months in after she accidentally spilled a pot of boiling oil over her left leg and became infirm. She wanted to help so badly but, like a cheap slapstick, kept failing in her efforts, hurting herself in the process. The pain she encountered by laboring wasn't the pain she philosophized about, which was more spiritual, less fleshy: It was a pain humiliating but not abject. So, like many other rich girls, she wrote instead.

Writing requires its own attention to pain, too, and I honed mine from early on. In losing myself in the mirror and then in hypnosis, I longed for a home, paying for it with an attention so totalizing I didn't know I was paying it at all. In throwing myself—physically, emotionally—into my writing, I avoided facing the inherited other hurts of my sister's loss. I see a parallel with Weil's work in this, a projection of pain outward and a close examination as it comes back again. Like mine, like my mother's, Weil's short life was one marked by a deeply political hunger for both beauty and faith. Through depriving herself until she disappeared, Weil believed, she would find God. Creation, she wrote, exists in God's absence.

This is the central idea of *Saint Maud*, as well—accessing the divine through unqualified punishment. In fact, the movie can be seen as both an embrace and a rebuke of Weil's ideas, filled with compassion and caution alike. "Never waste your pain," Maud says at the end of the film, shortly before she immolates.

When hypnotism didn't seem to work, I laughed it off. Privately, though, I was devastated—another way out had foreclosed itself to me. In response, I fulfilled my obligations like a robot: I went to dinner. I went to school. I went to Mass. I went to lay flowers on my sister's small flat grave every time we traveled through Richmond, and I held my mom afterward. In the wake of the loss I was born into, I felt such tremendous guilt—a guilt that led back to faith, like it did for her. I felt like my own pain was a mark of divine love. I felt like a saint, too.

By the end of high school, I'd taught myself how to hide my dissociations. I thought this a triumph that I could temporarily escape, undetected, from the crushing weight of my own self. But I didn't think of why I hungered for absence in the first place. I didn't think about how I only saw a woman in the mirror, the tightening in my chest I'd feel when I saw a particularly beautiful boy. I didn't think about *what* I hungered to hide, why I cringed when people called my name. Instead, I wore my bright gold cross necklace, bright as my hair, and tried to be the best little Catholic I could be. Maybe in this way, I knew how to mesmerize all along. Through how I attended to others, how I contorted myself to the desires of others, I was always already distracting myself from anything deeper. Through all these practices, I avoided confronting the reality of my body and, echoing what my faith taught me, of my body to come.

In fifth grade, staring into the mirror until I lost sight of myself, I entered trances for minutes at a time. I was there, I was there, and then—sudden as a flame licking a body—I was gone. The only thing left behind was my desperate belief that pain would save me, too. It would take me away from my own reflection, one that resembled my sister more than I felt comfortable admitting. I dissociated and then hurt myself to distract from what I feared I would become, and then dissociated once more from that hurt. I was bound by what was going to happen to me as sure as she was. The attention I paid was also a way to engage with the great, terrifying scope of the divine.

3.

I work through feelings by working through projects, and in 2021 I was focused on an oral history of Chrissy. Over Zoom, I'd interview my mother about my dead sister, talking for hours. I scanned documents from the cardboard box when I visited her, took pictures of the objects on the walls of our home.

When Chrissy was seventeen, she went to a center in Philadelphia to treat her bulimia, where she stayed for several months. The center was where she made the papier-mâché masks—the ones that still hang on my mother's walls—painted in dark blues and ochres and contoured around her Vaseline-slicked face. Chrissy made two masks, although her original plan was to make three, summing up all the ways she hid her personality stacked on top of one another. The happy mask, she planned, would cover up a second mask whose face twisted in a rictus of anger. It would only be once you removed that mask that you got to the real core of her, a face parched with tears. But she ran out of time when she was there so only completed the happy and angry masks. Then she died, and her sadness remained intangible still.

There's a long, intertwined history of deprivation and faith, ranging from the fasts we practiced during Lent to hunger strikes to more pernicious acts. Simone Weil was no exception to this history. She had an eating disorder, too—or, at least, appeared to abhor food and endorsed its absence. Hunger, she wrote, was a way of getting closer to God. "We have to fasten on to the hunger," she said, "Only the highest has the right to be satisfied." For her, not eating was a way of making herself more open to God's light; through the pain of that, too, she believed she could be transformed. This was how she died, in 1943: complications from a hunger strike that lined up with her larger philosophy anyway.

My own eating disorder had been much more minor, but I related to both my sister and Weil. I ran cross country, regularly finishing in third or fourth place among my team, and my body was a field of disappointments. I tried anything I could to wrest control away from it and back toward me; not eating was merely one way I could assert control, and the easiest one to practice. I skipped meals, cut deliberately small portions off pot roasts. Then, late at night, I'd sneak downstairs and devour one sticky peanut-butter sandwich after another, eating until I was full. My father saw me doing this once and laughed loudly when he did. "My growing boy," he said. In *Saint Maud*, there's a quieter link to food, but it's still there. "You must be the loneliest girl I've ever seen," the dancer says to Maud, as a birthday cake is brought in that neither character eats.

Around the same time Siobhan and I first watched the movie, I called the eating disorder clinic to ask for my sister's records of her stay there. I was nervous they'd deny me access, so I rehearsed all morning. *Hi. Can I talk to the record keeper? Yes, I'm next of kin.* I thought by understanding her relationship to food and what fueled that I could find another point of connection between us. But when they finally transferred me over, it turned out all that worrying was for nothing.

"I'm sorry dear," the receptionist said. "We only keep the records for fifteen years, and then we shred them." Chrissy stayed at the center in 1990; I was sixteen years too late. I hung up the phone, a familiar emptiness gnawing at my stomach. I hadn't eaten lunch yet, and it was almost dinner.

In the Catholic tradition there are mysteries, contradictions within the faith that are supposed to inspire more faith. They're divided into categories: The luminous mysteries, when Christ was on His missions. The sorrowful mysteries, when He was hung up on the cross and agonizingly died. We memorized each mystery in catechism class in preparation for Confirmation; you're supposed to recite them as you pray the rosary, and we knew there would be a test before we were confirmed. Memorizing wasn't hard, though; I was enraptured by the mysteries. Maybe it was the clearness of a biography told through acts and not belief alone. Each mystery seemed ancient, saying, *Here is every unknown thing we've seen. Now, build a faith out of them.* The faith in question was Catholicism, but other fraught things are created from good intentions every day, too. Hungers can be filled in many ways.

When my father died years later, faith was one of the few things he left behind. After the funeral, my mother gave me his wooden rosary, the heavy set of beads he purchased traveling through Venezuela in his thirties. "He would have wanted you to have this," she said. "He was a bastard, but he loved us." And he did, but I think he loved God more. After all, his favorite thing about me, I found out from a poem he published when I was still a child, *was* my faith. "He prayed," my father said, talking about me, "without me even asking him to. I truly think he's touched by God."

When I received the rosary, I closed the door to the guest room of what was now my mother's house alone, and I held the beads in my hand, trying to pray like I used to. But it had been years since I had gone to Mass, and even longer since I had held a rosary, and despite my best efforts, I remembered only several mysteries and a brief smattering of prayers. Everything I had memorized, from Christ's baptism to death, the accumulation of my mother's and my own devotion, had gone with him. Running my fingers across the polished wood, I knew that I wouldn't pick up Catholicism again, even in the wake of his death. In its place, there was just another absence.

So instead, I started to make up my own words for the rosary as I prayed. My father was cruel, but how much of that was bottled-up grief? Sure, he wanted my mother to shrink her own grief down to something controllable. Sure, he started yelling at both of us every time she'd fight back. But regardless of what he said when he was sober, several drinks in he'd always start crying, too. Fingering the beads, I recited a prayer to him of my own devising: *We didn't get along but I miss you still. I hope you went easily.* I paused. *I hope things are easier for both of us now that you're gone.* I paused again. *I hope you died without pain.*

One of the things so cruel about my father's email was how it foreclosed a greater kinship with my sister, and by extension anyone I shared kinship with. I looked like Chrissy, and the same traits stuck to us both. Who's to say she didn't influence what I became? Even our charts were in the same family—my Pisces, her Cancer, both our Gemini moons, swimming together. But if I think about Chrissy now, I just think about the viciousness of his words toward me, and his wife, and the daughter who wasn't biologically his but was his family nonetheless. I think of him—just as he, when he thought of her, thought of me.

My whole family did. It was part of our story. After all, my father was right—the link between me and her *was* the other faith I inherited, part of my hunger, too. He had three children of his own before he married my mother, and they drew their own connections between me and Chrissy. "Before I knew I was pregnant," my mother told me, several months before he died, "your older sister had a dream that Chrissy gave me a baby." She paused, took a drink of water. "And then I knew, and there you were."

4.

I don't believe in God anymore, at least not the Christian sort of God. Things aren't that simple. But when Siobhan visited me a year after we started flirting with each other again, I had started reclaiming faith, or at least the signifiers of it. A tiny crucifix, torn from a cheap rosary, above my stove. A golden thurible the size of my palm, dispensing frankincense throughout the living room. A book of saints that I flipped through every week, finding those who felt moved by

God to be better than themselves. I had just gotten out of the psych ward. This faith, it felt, was all I had.

"Wow," she said, laughing, as she dropped off her bags in my bedroom, "you weren't kidding about the ex-Catholic thing."

My favorite saint I discovered during this time was Agatha, the patron saint of an absurd amalgamation of causes: breast cancer patients and sexual assault survivors and earthquake victims as well. She, like most women saints, was tortured by pagans. Supposedly they wanted her to renounce her faith—something that pagans were always doing—and took her breasts in hot tongs. "Renounce God," they said, and the ground started to shake, and she said no. Then they took out a knife. "Renounce God," they said, and she said no, and in one fell swoop they cut off her breasts, and then an earthquake came and stopped the men from killing her outright.

What stuck with me the most about Agatha's life was the way she wasn't restored to former glory the same way other saints were. In most icons of her, she floats holding her severed breasts on a plate. Peace, God, whatever: I knew she was propaganda to prevent women from reacting more strongly to men's shit, but even still. The fact that something could be taken from her and she responded by putting her losses on display spoke to me before I even could register why.

In the psych ward, they told us to avoid more intense forms of self-harm. Instead, they said, it's better to hold ice cubes or dunk our heads in water. Pain was good, but smaller pains were better. "Suffering isn't noble," a worksheet we were given said. "Survival is." But instead of pain, I found myself most in moments of pain's aftermath, tracing open a flickering faith that never fully persisted. That was why I avoided eating until I felt sick. That was why in high school I had hit myself in the bathroom until I couldn't anymore. In the moments after I started to split open with hurt, I felt like I could see God or what was left behind when God left.

I was no longer hurting myself by the time Siobhan visited, but hurting myself was never really the point. I was looking for a way to feel closer to whoever I was most devoted to at the time. Simone Weil's work ensnared so much because it realized, like I hadn't yet at the time, that pain can be its own faith, its own misdirected love. *Saint Maud* spoke to me, too, because it argued both for and against the same thing. Yes, Maud kills and dies—but she truly loves her companion beforehand. She experiences an excess of faith, of desire, and finds herself through that until she doesn't.

"I love you," Siobhan said two days after she arrived. She said it after we finally, officially, broke up. It was on my couch, and the dim lamplight of the apartment caught in her lustrous brown eyes. We had realized shortly after the ex-Catholic thing that we didn't make sense as lovers anymore. We had both gotten out of other relationships, and we both needed time to grow, and change, away from our devotion to each other. "I promise we'll stay close," she said, and, as she became my ex-girlfriend again, I felt held in the light of that promise. Sitting on the couch together, our legs almost touched. The thurible in the corner puffed out thin clouds of Frankincense. And I felt aflame but also in control. As I started to cry again, Siobhan reached a hand around my shoulder. I was secure and in my late twenties, and I was with her, and I was alive, which is to say I was living the sort of life my sister never got to have. I was here—and she, like God, was not. My father was right to say that Chrissy made me. Without her, I would not have been born. I would not have loved. There would have just been her.

"I never wanted you to feel like I was trying to replace Chrissy with you," my mother said in one of our interviews. "So if I ever thought, *Oh my god, that's exactly like Chrissy*, I would keep that thought to myself."

Things we had in common:

- Our kindness to animals

- Our noses and our lips

- Our love of the sea

Even though we shared a mother, my mother was fifteen when my sister was born and thirty-eight when I was. Between that and how shaped by grief she was when I grew up, I don't think Chrissy and I even knew the same woman. Likewise, my father—Chrissy's stepfather—was transformed utterly by her death. He drank more heavily. He hid his emotions that weren't anger. "He was never the same," murmured a family friend once when we went to visit him in Tampa Bay—my father just out of earshot, refilling his wine glass in the kitchen. But my father never talked about his prior life, so I didn't even know what he was like before—only that I would dream of growing up unhaunted in a house in a city, filled with laughter and Chrissy alive and the children from my father's first marriage, instead of the echoey house in rural North Carolina that was ours. I would dream of a life with her.

The main way faith can develop is through absence. As often as the saints talked about epiphanies, bodies flooding with grace, it's far more common that faith appears after the hole does, water flooding into an already existing recess. I believe my parents tried to fill their own hole as well as they could. Hence my mother's stories, and my father's flood. That was my relationship to my sister, as told by them: I didn't know her, but in her absence, she shaped me. Her clothes, her features, their memories. Her pictures, her masks, our grief. All of this is to say she was a part of me, too. With her, I filled that hole with something like faith. I was the water, and I was the hole.

Chrissy wasn't religious specifically—even though she briefly wanted to become a nun. But she hadn't been *raised* religious, and I had. When she was eighteen, she thought about joining the military, something I was staunchly opposed to. She had hazel eyes, nothing like my cobalt. I didn't know who she would have turned into had she grown up into an adult, or how she loved when she wasn't in crisis. Even what her politics would be now are a mystery to me—it's entirely possible that had she lived, I would be disappointed in her like I've been disappointed in so many other people in my life. But I can't know that for sure, because if she were alive, I wouldn't be.

Things that were different:

- How quick she was to anger

- Her (much more intense) eating disorder

- Her family

My mother's favorite photo of Chrissy was one she no longer had in her possession but had been seared into her memory. It was a photo of her that her friends had placed into the coffin at the funeral. They had gone to the beach together the day the photo was taken, shortly before the car crash, and Chrissy gleamed in the sun, skin shimmering as copper and gold as her hair.

"She was holding up a sea creature," my mom said, "filled with wonder up until the very, very end."

5.

In the beginning of *Saint Maud*, which seized Siobhan and I around the same time I really started thinking about my relationship with my sister, Maud and the woman she takes care of have a transcendent experience. Sitting next to each other, they roll on the ground in ecstasy, filled with the grace of God or the sheer intoxication of each other. They're feeling what Maud says she feels in God's presence: "When He's pleased, it's like a shiver or sometimes it's like a pulsing. And it's all warm and good. And He's just there." As she talks, the two women hold hands, and in that moment of intimacy, there's nothing bad looming at all. The only shadows there are living ones.

Ultimately, I think it was the research that saved me. It was only when looking into my sister's life that I started to notice what I wanted: an ability to love who I was without punishing myself in the interim, an ability to love others also. I was so fixated on loss that I didn't realize how much I needed myself—the others I loved, and the me I would love, too. I was so dedicated to solving her life, I almost didn't notice the changes happening in my own as well.

On the last day of Siobhan's stay in my apartment, she gave me a tattoo. She promised to do this when we'd dated years ago, but I was still too unsure of our relationship then to commit to something that permanent. Besides, I didn't know what I wanted. When she was there again, though, I had a clear request: an engraving, in cursive script, of my favorite artist's de facto last statement. So my ex left my place in Flatbush in the morning and took the subway up to Bushwick to borrow tattooing materials from the friend she traveled with. By the time she got back, it was midafternoon, and we cleaned the glass coffee table and stretched Saran Wrap over everything. It took just half an hour and then we were done, the letters curved on my leg, shining bright and still raised to the touch.

A month earlier, I had gotten a tattoo of Saint Agatha holding her breasts on a tray in her right hand and a feather in her left. The tattoo was in the style of an engraving, thin hatched lines spiderwebbing across my thigh, but now illuminated by the words Siobhan tattooed above, it transformed, blossoming out into a new context. I didn't even think of her tattoo and Saint Agatha interacting, but they're almost close enough to touch. In the years since, everyone assumes it is a singular tattoo; they send a coherent message together, one of survival and care and what we do with what's been done to us. If the tattoos were people, they'd breathe the same air, huddle under the same blanket. They'd have the same nose, same lips.

It's just two words—*Love me*—but billowing out above Saint Agatha's slightly smiling face they still make a private language marking my leg in care and lust and blood, talking to God or maybe Siobhan or my sister or maybe me or maybe there's no difference between any of them. Regardless, Siobhan's handwriting is embedded in me now, echoing what the artist Greer Lankton wrote inside every artwork she made and what I've written this whole book to say.

I hope my sister was cared for. I hope in past relationships—before the cheating, before the suspicions—she felt as held as I did in that moment, my ex's hands dancing again up my leg like nothing had changed.

I said the first photo ever taken of me was in the water, but there's one maybe even before then. It's undated and at Chrissy's grave, a short thumbnail tombstone close to the ground. My mother hunches behind the stone, trimming the rose bush tangled there. In the foreground I am mid-crawl, several months old, wearing a navy-blue unisex jumpsuit similar to what I'm wearing now. My hair pokes up in a cowlicked blond sprawl, and in the picture, I hover in front of the grave, right over where my sister's body would be.

Here are the facts: I had a sister who loved with fierceness and abundance, who loved her family dog with a passion, and whose face creased with joy at seeing sea creatures. She was an easy baby, one who never cried. She cared about everyone she met, regardless of how much she was hurt by them. When she died, I was born.

Growing up, I didn't realize how much she shaped me. I lost myself in my father's faith, but also hers. And then I changed that faith when I found myself again. That's the thing: You can't have growth without something being left behind. Is it any wonder I imprinted on the women pierced by Catholicism and loss in the same way I was? Is it any wonder *Saint Maud* was so important to me, too? Here was a film about desiring—not God, but anything that could fill a void. It was 2021. Siobhan and I watched the film in silence. A back bending in half as a woman floated upside down. An act of care, God's grace shared on the floor together. A digital whine, a spark of flame, a continuum between the past and now. A history.

As the movie ended, Siobhan and I looked into each other's eyes, and then she exited out of the Zoom window. In the dimmed laptop screen, I saw my eyes alone; drained of color, they looked like my sister's or Siobhan's or both. Sometimes connection, not suffering, gets us closer to God, too. Sometimes a religion or a relationship are only what fills a hole until something better comes along. I never met my sister, but still I've tried to live my life fully in the light of the love that everyone who survived felt for her. In the moments before the car hit the ice, I hope she had faith in that, too.

Crazy in Love

1.

My first visit to the psych ward, I was fifteen years old. Rather, it was a psych ward turned student dormitory. I went to the residential high school in Durham, built in a refurbished hospital, because it was free to everyone and the easiest way to get away. There, ghost stories were told incessantly on campus, and students spoke of different wings of the school in hushed tones. The morgue obviously was haunted, as was the tunnel leading from the squat English building to the main lobby. Even the art there was marked by the past, a hideous twisted metal heap of a sculpture sitting squat on the front lawn that school legend said had been willed there by a peeved alum. We lived amid all of this: The girls' dormitories were in the wing of the building that contained not just the psych ward but the former morgue as well. In contrast, the boys' dormitories, where I lived, were a concrete slab of gentrifier-chic architecture built in the past fifteen years, and there were no ghosts there at all except us. For two years, we walked down long winding glass halls, pulled all-nighters in cement tombs, gulped down caffeine pills in the cavernous cafeteria; and as unsafe as it felt at times, it was home.

I didn't yet have the framework to understand myself as crazy at the time, so when I flunked out of two of my classes and, subsequently, the high school itself, I had no clue why it had happened. I felt sad hearing about my looming expulsion, but, in a way, it was my constant state of sadness that caused the flunking, not the other way around. And yes, if I'm being precise, it's more likely the accumulation of what happened earlier in my life that caused the ripple effect of sadness to expulsion, but I'm less interested in the ghosts of my past than I am in what came next.

Flunking out wasn't my first experience with failure—I ran cross-country, despite not being great at it, so I had already acclimated to the soft disappointment of a middle-of-the-pack finish—but it was, at the time, my most serious one. I contested my expulsion at a formal hearing in the dead of winter in front of a panel of balding men in ill-fitting suits. Out of desperation, I tried to articulate a depression inarticulable in its depths. Over the course of my several-hours-long hearing, I talked about my sudden mood swings, how I would start crying and be unable to stop for hours; the general sense of doom that filled my bones; my lack of motivation that whole winter to do anything. I left out how I would crawl under the sinks in the shared bathrooms at 3 a.m. so my roommate wouldn't notice me punching myself in the gut over and over again until it bruised; or how, when I was touched, I would freeze up completely, throat closing during sex so I often couldn't say no even if I wanted to.

Fucking was technically forbidden at the school, although everyone did it, sneaking into dorm room bedrooms late at night or onto the math hall on weekends. I lost my virginity to my first girlfriend in the third-floor music wing bathroom, checkered tiles cold and sticky against my ass. She came before I did, and I felt, briefly, a trickle of success before the familiar deep, empty feeling I was used to washed over me again. We met up every evening until we didn't; I ate her out until she'd come and then would anxiously shut down when she touched me in return. She was a Republican and we had nothing in common besides both being sixteen; of course we didn't last.

At the time of my expulsion, I was in the middle of weathering my first breakup and—like most first heartbreaks—I had convinced myself that I would be unalterably alone forever. My ex had cheated on me with a greasy leather jacket–wearing military brat and open racist who taunted me before my Chinese final exam. In response, I pinned him against a brick wall in the cafeteria and started punching. As I hit him, I felt like I was coming into myself, at home in my body at last; I felt like I was a man, as my father had willed me to be. When I was done, people cheered, but after the compliments died down, I once again felt empty. The sudden thrum of violence did nothing to hush the 24/7 buzz of anxieties around our incipient breakup. Hurting myself was the only way I could get it to quiet.

In response to my partial disclosure, the men at the residential school conditionally readmitted me—sentencing me to remedial classes, study hall on weekends, and, once a week, therapy at a clinic several blocks away from school. My GPA took a hit, nuking my chances of getting into the colleges I wanted to, but all told, I got off easy; many students I knew weren't let back in at all, especially after the weed bust at the start of the year basically wiped out half my dormitory.

I was supposed to ask for an escort to go to therapy, as we weren't allowed off campus on our own, but usually I chose to sneak off, squat-running past the chain-link perimeter fence until I was sure no one was tailing me. After sessions with Dr. Jen, I would walk down Broad Street toward campus, slurping down lavender milkshakes and stopping in record stores to pick up punk vinyl. I could get expelled if I was caught off campus alone, so I'd dip into an alley whenever I saw residential advisors strolling down the street, keys jangling off a school-issued carabiner telegraphing their presence before I even saw their bright blue R.A. polos.

I told the therapist almost nothing about what I actually felt: The seismic waves of self-loathing I swam in at all times, the flashbacks I'd see when I'd close my eyes. I didn't tell my friends, either; I assumed the feelings were normal, and therefore boring. I didn't tell them how

I hurt myself. I didn't tell them why I couldn't sleep at night. I only confided my true feelings to a person in my hall who would, one week before graduation, jerk me off as I said no, please, stop.

Mainly, I talked to my therapist about academics. At the boarding school, we were crammed together taking college-level classes for two whole years, and all my energy went to trying to succeed at things I had no aptitude for. I fumbled anatomy and physics practicals and wrote incomprehensible notes in chemistry, barely scraping by with a C-minus off the grace of participation points despite getting Ds on almost all my exams. It wasn't just me who was overwhelmed in the school; even my peers who did well in STEM hurried around dripping with flop-sweat, chugging cup after cup of bitter cafeteria coffee. *Choose two*, the joke at the school went, *sleep, a social life, or good grades*, but I felt like I was failing at all three.

The only respite I had was in my relationships, which I entered with abandon, fucking in the hallways or the woods at the corner of campus daily, assuming if I could make others feel good, it would somehow rub off on me, too. All told, I was single for a month my senior year, replacing the Republican almost immediately with a girl who wore slouchy jeans and sundresses, almond-colored eyes bright with want whenever we saw each other.

Fucking, I thought, was a more effective way of hiding yourself than talking, and because of that it would take years before I would actually get close to anyone I slept with. Instead, my partners would come and I would come and I'd sneak back into the dorm late at night to punch myself again until I felt something. I only wanted to be normal and would do anything to appear as such. Most of the time, orgasms didn't require conversation. (Sure, I talked during sex as a teenager, but not often, and certainly not when in a state of my own overwhelm.) Instead, from my readmittance onward, I set a fixed pattern in my intimate life that I refused to diverge from; for the next eleven years, I hid and fucked and hid and fucked—passing wordless orgasms back and forth—until I hurtled onto the flickering fluorescent hallways of the psych ward. I didn't realize I was falling apart until it already happened.

2.

Shortly after my readmission to the school, I bought the DVD of Lars von Trier's *Antichrist* from the FYE at the mall up the road, lying about my age to get the NC-17 rated film. The movie was immediately controversial upon its release that year, prompting a mass walkout at Cannes and a critical pillorying once it hit limited release. But something about the trailer, which an edgelord friend showed me on YouTube, spoke to me.

It was a time of hope, which I distrusted, and maybe the movie's cynicism was what sold me on it. Barack Obama had just won the Nobel Peace Prize. Pundits were talking about the war finally ending. The Black Eyed Peas were busy making dance tracks for optimists, and "I Gotta Feeling" blared from every radio I heard or dance party I went to. Everyone was looking for a *good time* then, and *Antichrist* seemed decidedly not that—which made it feel truer. The trailer promised a talking disemboweled fox and full-penetration sex scenes and Charlotte Gainsbourg writhing in agony as Willem Dafoe loomed over her. I felt bad all the time and hungered for something that spoke to those emotions. So, I popped the DVD into my laptop after midnight on a Tuesday, headphones on so my roommate wouldn't hear, and once I finished, I immediately started the film again.

I watched it twice the first night, and then again several weeks afterward. Then, over the last trimester of school (classes at this school were split into trimesters, not semesters; even the course load labored under the principle of *more is more*) I lent the DVD out to as many people as I could. I knew I could pull off a fucked-up *have you seen this?* pose and most people would be intrigued off that alone. *The Human Centipede* and *American Psycho* were circulating dorms, and the cinnamon challenge—can you snort a spoonful of cinnamon without throwing up?—had just spread like a plague. When we weren't cramming, students swapped tests of endurance weekly, so I played up the moments of gored excess when I hyped the film—describing in detail a penis spurting bloody jism at the moment of ejaculation, clitoral lips cut off with a pair of kitchen shears, a millstone driven through a human leg.

But the truth was, I never liked gore for gore's sake, and only watched *The Human Centipede* because I thought I could trick myself into feeling something through it. The scenes I described to friends over dinners or late at night, I didn't even watch; when the bodily mutilation started in *Antichrist*, I'd look away, tab over to my internet browser or doodle faces in a notebook instead. It was the rest of the movie that spoke to me.

When it came out, almost everyone described *Antichrist* as a misogynistic film: woman loses child, woman goes crazy, therapist husband kills her and escapes and is then haunted by her ghost at the end. A pop feminism had started to reenter the collective consciousness, in part why critics loathed it. But I related to Charlotte Gainsbourg's character, a crazy woman, like few protagonists I had seen before. She cried like I cried, winced in pain with no explicit cause like I did. Her relationship was falling apart, too, because of grief and her husband's bad decisions.

"What's wrong with me?" she yelled, and I heard the question like a cloudburst. I couldn't say "that's me," because I knew how that would sound even then—insane—but as I rewatched it, I found a power in what I didn't recognize yet as sisterhood.

The history of mental illness in women is often one of patriarchal manipulation: Zelda Fitzgerald being confined to a sanitorium by her plagiarist husband F. Scott; the diagnosis of hysteria in general and its indebtedness to the idea of the "wandering womb," a persistent idea that a woman's uterus can move around and cause distemper not experienced in men; the frequent dismissal of testimony from abuse survivors, often women, as deranged rantings.

It was in my family, too. At night, my father, usually several drinks in, would chastise anyone he deemed a "crazy bitch," a category that more often than not included my mother, a woman who threw plates and called him on his shit but also loved with a fierceness I didn't see from anyone else. Even now, the "dangerous" diagnoses, such as borderline or other personality disorders—i.e., the diagnoses I received at the ward—are doled out to women more frequently than men. There's a gynophobia at the heart of this that would seem to exclude trans women, but we're considered crazy, too, even more so. Gender identity disorder was in the DSM until 2013. Even now, our rights are being stripped away everywhere.

But if women are labeled crazy more often, we are made crazy, too. I can accept that calling others crazy is a form of social control, but that doesn't change the reality of my own shifting moods, racing thoughts, inability to trust others, fits of dissociation. It doesn't change the fact that at various points, I have been very much not well. I'm bored of the narrative that says I'm the way I am only because of *what happened to me*, but I'd be a fool to not acknowledge the impact every forced entry or bruise has had on my mental health. This—the steady stripping of a woman's sanity, to the point that she becomes disposable—is the plot of *Antichrist*, to a T.

"Honesty is the best policy" goes the refrain from people who can trust their own brains. But I never even tried being honest, and certainly never tried it with those similar to me. Through high school and later, I practiced solitude, isolation, and deception and thought it a solution. I hid myself from those I could see a part of me in, plunged into relationships where I wouldn't have to disclose anything. That changed several years ago, though. Now, I want to find solidarity not just in my mental illness, but in sharing space with those like me as well. Now I believe in love as strength, not just a way to hide. Every time I enter a new coupling, I ask myself the question I should have been asking from the beginning: How do you love as a crazy woman? How do you love other crazy women, too?

I rewatched *Antichrist* a decade later with Vespertine, someone I had newly become friends with. I cautioned her about the scenes of intense violence at the end, finger hovering over the fast forward button on the Roku. We skipped past the clitorectomy, but she loved the movie as much as I did, maybe even more, eyes wide and engaged through the whole thing. Charlotte Gainsbourg's character wailed as she injured herself again and again, and as we watched, we felt that bright unsteady thrill of representation.

As the film went on, slowly our hands crept across the couch toward each other; an arm interlocked, then a calf extended over another. "That movie was so good," she said, and then, "I'd be down to stay a bit later," quietly, as I looked at her. It was after midnight. Her eyes opened wide and she blinked them slowly. Both our lips were slightly wet, beginning to purse, and because it was autumn and just starting to chill, my knit wool blanket sat only partially around our legs. A thin trickle of weed smoke from earlier hung in the air. When we fucked later that night, our breath was heavy with it.

In high school, whenever I talked about my past, I would talk about it as something *common*, a kind of understatement intended to make me feel less alone. My father beat me across the room only once, I said to a table of friends, which is better than most. I'm lucky. Everyone looked away.

I still have that same tendency to look for kinship in the wounds of others, and this is what brought Vespertine and me closer together. Even now, I divulge my own pain only in situations where it seems

I might get a similar confession in return. I feign or find twinness in moments of intimacy, a way of preempting the aloneness and distance within me even when I'm surrounded by friends. Like many of my avoidant tendencies, I learned this at the school.

But with Vespertine, I didn't have to feign this sharedness; it was already there. We bonded over our unpleasant experiences in our shared MFA program, the books and songs and musicians—Warren Zevon, Cat Power, Townes Van Zandt—we both loved, how swiftly we could spiral into paranoia or untraceable fear. We had the same diagnoses slid our way by apathetic or overly salvational psychiatrists, and we bonded over that, too, treated each word on our respective charts with skepticism or a tentative and trembling acknowledgment. Our diagnoses were like astrological signs for us: They meant both everything and nothing at the same time. When she came the first time, her mouth opened round as a peach pit and I came right afterward, quieter and more withdrawn, and then we held each other, two trans women pressed so tight our stomachs touched, a constellation of scratch marks fading and hickeys ripening across our bodies, bedsheets twisted around us, and it felt like an arrival.

Vespertine and I started dating after watching *Antichrist*, the same film that drove so many people away when it was released. After the movie, we started seeing each other sporadically as you do in New York mid-pandemic—every other Saturday, or a Tuesday night we didn't have other plans—in a way that wasn't a warning sign at the time. We texted almost every day, though. At the beginning she would wait a full afternoon—almost a full week by the end—to respond to texts, but would tweet about me in the interim, which thrilled and frightened me. *Had my best date in years*, she tweeted. *Thinking about my crush*. Once, cryptically, *being in a relationship that scares you is a source of strength*.

"We are the same," she said toward the end; "that's what scares me." But she was rich, and I wasn't. She had been institutionalized several times, and I had not. She would vanish for days at a time and when she reappeared would whisper delicately, "I really like you." A month into our seeing each other, she went to the psych ward again, three weeks in Bellevue and a smattering of emails until we saw each other again. I felt like I had to show up for her. I loved it.

"Sweetie," my mom said on the phone one day, "are you sure this relationship is good for you?"

"Of course it is," I snapped, but she had a right to ask. It was my first relationship as a politicized crazy person dating another crazy person, and I was drunk off it. I played up our similarities, ignored moments of conflict or how I felt when she ghosted me for days at a time. No, the relationship was good, I thought, and I was glad to be in it, even when I wasn't. We were like each other, and that made our love safe.

Circumstance had something to do with how I felt for Vespertine. The previous year and a half of the pandemic had driven me monogamous—apart from a flirtation with an ex on the other side of the country—and the sudden branching open of options I saw with Vespertine was intoxicating and immediate. I felt cared for, or like there was the potential to be cared for, in a way I hadn't since the pandemic started. But mainly, I fell hard like I hadn't in years. She was all I could think about. In fact, I started this essay in the thick of it, when we were still dating. The distance I'm feigning now doesn't even exist.

3.

The high school therapist, my first official one, was like many to come: uncomfortably cheerful and mildly indifferent, office filled with tchotchkes and minimalist wall art. By our second session, she turned to me and said, "I think you have ADHD. Do you mind if I write you a prescription?"

I went to her for depression but telling her that necessitated telling her about what I did away from classes, which I refused to do. Instead, I mentioned falling half-asleep in courses and difficulty paying attention, leaving out the fact that I stayed up till 4 a.m. punishing myself for perceived sins, unwittingly playing the role of the grief-shadowed Catholic I had been raised to be. I hated the way the pills, small and white, made me feel—disconnected from my emotions, only a vague irritability left behind. I wanted my sadness to stop, but not like that; under Mydayis, which wasn't even supposed to treat my emotions, I turned into a frozen lake. I stopped crying and hitting myself, but that probably resulted more from an inchoate drive to improve myself than the meds themselves. Regardless, the therapist didn't know about any of this. I stopped taking the meds weeks later and told her that everything had become well at last. I had started dating someone else, a girl whose father had died in a highway accident the previous year and was struggling with her own mental health. My problems, I thought, could be overshadowed by hers. I had no need for my therapist to interrogate me further. Comparatively, I told myself, I was healed.

But I ignored the full scope of my own history. After all, the first time I went crazy wasn't in high school. It was in kindergarten. That winter, we had flown out of Pennsylvania to a rich family friend's condo in Tampa. The friend had dropped out of seminary to be a realtor—its own abandonment of religious faith for the illustrious temple of capitalism. The walls of his place shone brighter white than anything I had seen before, and he lived casual with money in a way my parents did not, had never. We spent a week in Tampa with him, soaking in the same climate I was born in, and I waded into the crystal blue water every day, battered gold by the sun. I laughed on the beach as my parents drank merlot and threw down hands of rummy, happy in a way that felt overwhelming, uncontrollable. And then I went back home and resumed my mean little friendships and everything clicked shut.

I called it "Tampa Bay Sickness" because I didn't know what else it could be: Food lost its taste in my mouth and the gray Pennsylvania weather turned unfriendly and hostile. All of a sudden, I couldn't read, could barely speak, lost my motivation for anything. Instead, for months I cried, balling myself up on the checkered green and yellow carpet of the Montessori school I attended. I couldn't articulate what was wrong with me. I felt buffeted by my feelings, pushed in all directions by some malevolent figure pulling the strings inside my heart.

Because it was a Montessori, one of my teachers—Dan, a man with crinkly eyes and a great white beard whose head scraped the entrance of the building—accommodated my moods as best he could. But most of my other instructors were less forgiving. "Your child has to do work," my mother remembers one of the teachers telling her at a parent-teacher conference; "you're *spoiling* him." I couldn't do work; I could only stare out the windows, blank inside.

Dan, though, gave me a corner of the room to retreat to and some counting blocks to distract myself with when I got too overwhelmed. Maybe he thought this would inspire me to reengage with my studies, but even then, I didn't complete any schoolwork for a whole long winter. Instead, I tried my hardest just to hold on to life. I stared out the window; I cried; I hid from the shatter of plates during my parents' fights when I was home; I saw Jimmy.

When spring came and graduation from kindergarten was in sight, my mood started to lift, and I could engage with the outside world again. I began to smile again. I completed assignments. My parents' fighting would continue, but it stopped bothering me as much, and as I moved into first grade, I stopped spending time with my first abusive friend. For years, I pretended that first spate of sadness never happened; when I thought of it, I thought it an anomaly. *I was sick, but now I'm better* became the refrain. I didn't even tell my high school therapist about it; I just received the pills she gave me, and smiled, and disregarded usage instructions. *I'm different from other people*, I'd say, as I set the pills aside; *I can handle my problems on my own*. In session—just like in my expulsion hearing—I'd lie by omission about my sudden mood shifts, how quickly melancholy would overtake me. I'd never mentioned the familiar feeling of retreating into my body during sex, vision compressing into fragments as if through a pinhole camera: a finger, a tooth, a tongue.

I continued this for years, often not even knowing I was lying; I just felt desperation at disappointing anyone in my life with less than stellar progress and comported myself accordingly. Chastised by flunking out of the residential school, I wanted to be the best pupil imaginable, the best friend, the best lover, and would hide anything that interrupted my ability to be seen as such. It's surprising it took me until 2021 to be committed, but that just spoke to how good at masking I really was.

Masking, of course, is another form of closeting: I pretend to be this so you won't know I'm really that. It's also a capitulation to an oppressive world: "Masking," notes social psychologist Devon Price in his book *Unmasking Autism*, "is a state of exclusion forced onto us from the outside." It was no wonder I was good at it; I built up an entire skill set around hiding—one that I perfected in high school but practiced all the way back to elementary school. I learned quickly to hide, ceased displaying my sadness as publicly after Tampa Bay Sickness, and started hiding my own autism shortly afterwards. I covered it up, just as that world had taught me. Like my sister before, I put on my own masks and disappeared.

After I skipped fourth grade into fifth, the teacher pulled me aside and told me I'd be starting group meetings with the school counselor. I wasn't adjusting as smoothly as I could have, she said; I was acting out in class and shying away from people outside. The seams were showing. Her office was a yellow room across from the cafeteria, and we met for sixty minutes a day, twice a week. I was excused from social studies class for the occasion.

The office was decently sized, but our meetings felt cramped. There were just too many of us crammed in there, a whole folding table of problem children in between puppets hanging from long hooks and plasticky laminated "You're Capable of Anything!" posters puttied onto painted cinder-block walls. While I attended ostensibly for behavioral issues, the counselor never specified what they were. We were all there for that vague dx, but some problems showed up more explicitly than others. One girl who lived up the road from me with her grandmother wouldn't quit biting other people; one boy, a friend of mine, changed his name every few months and talked about not feeling safe in his own home. After I started attending, he stopped talking to me outside the room—ashamed of what we had in common? But I never asked him why our friendship had ended. I felt ashamed, too.

The counselor who gathered us wore loose burgundy turtlenecks and white slacks, our school colors. She held a little pad in her hand, which she'd occasionally scribble in with a nub of a pencil: An easel greeted us with a "how are you feeling?" in 72-point Impact and a series of faces for each respective mood. We'd hold them up on popsicle sticks, and she'd coo, "Good job!" as we mechanically lifted up a bland aspartame smiley or frowny face each session. The room smelled like dried-out glue sticks.

Her program promised intimacy and immediacy of feelings, but more specifically it promised assimilation. We watched an animated video where a boss yelled at his worker, who yelled at his wife, who went outside and kicked their dog. "End the cycle of violence," it said, but never told us what to do with those feelings instead. So, I lied, hiding my feelings but also my environment. No history of violence. No history of sexuality. "Everything's fine," I said, because I thought it was. The earlier moments—Jimmy suddenly turning on me and my memory going black; the rage seeping out of my father several drinks into every evening fogging over everything in our home; the closed-fist blows and kicks and stolen books and ruined clothes doled out to me by my peers each week; Tampa Bay Sickness—I thought they were what everyone went through.

And so, as the year slumped on, I lied more and more. "I love the fifth grade," I said, "I have so many friends. Here, I finally feel home."

Inside the yellow room, we didn't talk about hiding, didn't talk about pride. We just talked about normalcy, and how to ape it if we didn't feel it intuitively. In response, every week I'd hold up a wide smiley face on its wooden stick when we did our emotional go-round.

"Again?" the counselor would ask, and I'd say, with a chipper grin, "Can't complain!"

Home was a morass of stresses: My father's bladder cancer, which he discovered when I was in the first grade after I accidentally kicked him in the balls and he started pissing blood, seemed on the verge of returning. My parents, whose marriage was turbulent from my sister's death until my father's, were considering a separation. Several nights a week, I'd thrash in my sleep and wake up wedged between the bed and the wall, as if trying to make myself as small as possible. But inside the counselor's room, I spent my time compressing everything with the alacrity of a jeweler, fitting diamonds that reflected a happy, positive attitude into a display case and chucking the ones with flaws. My trash cans were overflowing.

At the end of the school year, the counselor gave everyone a computer-printout certificate of graduation. The toner was low so the colors were weird, all cyans and bright magentas. On mine, my last name was misspelled, a z where the s should be. "I'm so glad you've been making progress," said the counselor as she handed it to me, beaming. "You should be so proud of the work that you've done."

And then the summer happened, and the next school year was there. The program didn't continue, and I distinctly remember thinking: *I am free.*

4.

"You know Vespertine's cheating on you, right?" a friend blurted out over drinks, several months after we had started seeing each other.

I didn't. Suddenly, things made more sense—the long silences between text messages, how hot and cold she was with me, how she sometimes didn't even meet my eye when I arrived at her apartment. Vespertine, I learned, cheated in the queer New York polyamorous way where you have multiple partners but never tell them about each other. ("I didn't think I had to tell," she said on our phone call that following day. "If you hadn't found out, I wouldn't have.") I had been dating someone else, too, but told Vespertine about it from the jump, "Which made a difference," I said tearily on the phone.

The first time we fucked, I had seen huge slices running across Vespertine's arms and legs, wounds she glued and then sewed back up herself. They were deep red and keratinized, shocking against her light skin, and we never talked about what she did, but I felt seen in her as I'm sure she did in me. Being hurt probably gave Vespertine some license to hurt others, although I don't think that was what she was intentionally doing. Maybe the two were just concurrent travelers when we met and were dating.

It wasn't long into dating her that I started cutting myself, too, ribboning open my thighs with X-ACTOs in short bursts and slicing carefully around my tattoos. I would text her, wait for a response that never came, and carve into myself to make me feel better. Just as she hid her infidelities, I hid this from her. It wasn't just her who inspired me to do this; I had just seen *Secretary* with my other partner Avery, focused on the little kit of razors Maggie Gyllenhaal carried around to harm herself with. I connected immediately to her character—I found familiarity in similar relationships I had been practicing for several years, and loved that her dom, James Spader's character, was as nervous as she was. With time, I've grown more suspicious of the shaky, fallacious parallel the movie risks drawing between self-harm and sexualized pain. But when I saw it initially, I connected with Gyllenhaal's character's hunger for anything that would make her ache less; I saw her cutting, however self-destructive as it may be, as a panacea for me, too. I was underdosed on Lexapro and nothing seemed to help. *Maybe this is the solution*, I thought as I watched. I didn't think about exiting my relationship with Vespertine, which only made me feel unhappy, or about Avery and the things I hid from them, too. Instead, a week later, I took an X-ACTO knife to my leg and for the next month-plus, kept taking.

"I'm at rock bottom," Vespertine said finally, after I confronted her about the cheating. Before our long conversation, I pressed a finger into one of my scratches, and then picked up the phone. She was quiet and staticky across the line. Over the course of an hour and a half, I learned that she had just broken up with her best friend, and two of her longest-lasting exes had cut off contact with her. She had no friends, she said; she just had me, and the other people she saw. "But," she said, "I feel I can share this with you, not others. You were the only one I told about the ward."

As we talked, I was hurtling toward another breakdown, the worst I had ever had, the one that would land me, at last, in the psych ward as well. I was still too fixated on the fear of being alone to even realize the ways we had already hurt each other or the ways we would to come. I was too afraid to think of why my stomach sank when I even thought of seeing her again, the ways maybe we were making each other worse. I was too frightened to reflect on if I even wanted it at all.

I didn't mention any of this to her. Instead, I smiled and cleared my throat. "I want to make it work," I told her. "I want to see you again soon."

There's a photo on my phone that I took during the worst of it. It was the night after Avery was checked into the hospital with acute respiratory failure and the year's most brutal COVID surge had started hitting New York and my new meds, a similarly low-dosed replacement for Lexapro, were increasing my fears somehow. That week there was radio silence from Vespertine again, although she would emphasize the next time we talked how much she cared for me.

In the photo, my hair is a snared mess, both tangled and limp, and my eyeliner is running, face ruddy. I clearly have been crying. I don't want to say that I sliced myself up, or how. I don't want to add any details that would glamorize the moment, even if I tried to do so at the time. I'll just say that the blood was deep and red, and I smeared what was left afterwards on my mouth like lipstick.

In the picture, I'm posing in my underwear and a long-sleeve striped black-and-white top, thin outline of my genitals visible. My left leg bends to the camera, showing off what I did, and my eyes are almost closed. There's an intimacy there, but an uncomfortable one; the blood in the photo is still fresh. It's a selfie, taken in the mirror I had just gotten months earlier, bright gold edges lining the frame of the picture. Weeks earlier, I had stared at my reflection for hours in that mirror, tracing the beveled and curlicued edges of its embellished frame as I drank my body in with my eyes. Weeks before that, Vespertine and I posed in the same frame. *You're beautiful*, I'd whisper, until it sounded true. In the picture I tried to do the same thing, find a beauty in a moment of pain incomprehensible to me otherwise. I don't even remember cutting myself: just its bright, documented aftermath.

During this sudden unsteady collapse of a sudden unsteady relationship, I'd wake up and see faces on popsicle sticks all over. I'd dream of them, hurtling backward till I was in the fifth grade again. Happy, sad, happy, sad, happy, sad, like my sister's masks hanging on the living room wall. Over the eighteen years since, I had learned to fake it until I built a whole house out of my fakery: legs bloodied and smeared, ribs protruding under my collared top, windows gored red. I built the house, and then, aching and still lying to myself at twenty-seven, I shut myself inside and locked the door.

5.

My favorite moment in *Antichrist*: Charlotte Gainsbourg shivering in a meadow, unable to walk across. "It's just grass," her therapist husband says, voice harsh with irritation. "No," she says, "it *burns*." And then a few scenes later, suddenly free of pain, she crosses the whole field, beaming all the while. Pain is shaped, foremost, by its perspective.

"It's beautiful," Vespertine had whispered as we first watched *Antichrist* together, watching a woman's slow breakdown onscreen while almost holding hands. "It's beautiful."

One more bit of history: When I was in my sophomore year of college, my friend Zacharias was admitted to a psych ward. It was the first time I thought about one outside of the context of horror movies. We met at Occupy and held hands protesting the Dominion pipeline in western North Carolina, but after winter break, he disappeared suddenly. A week later we found out where to, a locked facility near his mom's house in Virginia Beach. Several organizing friends and my partner, the short butch with choppy orange hair and pilgrim steppers, caravanned up with me to Zach's home once they released him. I brought a mix CD, an image from a children's book of a toddler pointing a cork gun at a monster in his closet pasted onto the cover. "Go away, Nightmare, or I'll shoot you," was the caption underneath it.

Zach waited for us in his childhood bedroom, sitting crisscross applesauce under a torn La Dispute poster. He palmed a Dr Pepper with shaky hands, eyes smudged with circles, but smiled a wan smile when we clomped upstairs. "Let's go to the beach," someone said, and we piled into our van and drove down to the shore.

"It was a psych ward, you know?" Zach told me. I didn't. Most of my friends cut themselves, confessed drunkenly how little they wanted to be alive; that was one of the reasons we were able to dedicate ourselves to the cause so easily. But apart from Zach, I didn't know anyone who had been committed, or at least talked about it. No one spoke openly about psychiatric disability: It was always a whisper or darting rumor over anything else. Zach, though, was crazy and said so. I envied how directly he seemed to talk about his fears of losing control completely.

Bundled up in our coats, the wind cut at us, and the frozen sand crunched hard beneath our boots. Zach eventually dropped out of school, moved across the country, and we lost touch. But back then we were still close, two queer kids walking in unison down the beach with the rest of our friends tagging just slightly behind. "I'm out," he said quietly to me, and a flicker of something—maybe joy, or maybe just a brief lowering of his guard—crossed his face. I pulled him into a hug, and, hands nearly touching, we continued walking toward the horizon of the choppy surf.

During the breakup with Vespertine, it was winter again, and I biked down to Coney Island almost every day. I'd sit on the breakers, clamber over ice-slick rocks in my peacoat and mittens, ritualize my own walks up and down the beach. It seemed like our relationship had been all conflict: the cheating and the long phone call we had about it, but also a moment during sex a month earlier where she asked to stop and then started pressing against me and I panicked and suppressed it and tried to follow her lead as we started again and I asked her if it was okay that I was touching her and she said *yes* when she meant to say *no* and then fell asleep with my fingers inside her, body plunging into shock as things shuddered immediately again to a halt. I stopped on the beach and smoked an herbal cigarette, checked my phone for texts.

There's an unfairness in writing about any of this. These were pained people, and while their pain felt at times parallel to mine, it was not my own. But I thought if I saw a pain and named it, I could name myself as well. I was in it in a way I still risk being in it now, the fear of a breakup looming larger than a breakup itself, the fear of a conversation scarier than naming a thing outright. I didn't want to be alone, but I hid the whole time, so functionally I was.

"Let's talk about our issues later," I said on my last date with Vespertine, but we never wound up talking about anything after that—which surely was intentional on one of our parts. We shared diagnoses, but beyond that barely knew each other; we'd get high, fuck, watch movies, but talked only briefly about what we'd endured. "I'm scared," she said, and I felt scared, too, but never let her know.

It wasn't just her, but the rest of them, a whole pattern: Vespertine was part of a processional going back to high school, the nest of partners and relationships I forged when I could barely connect to myself. My high school girlfriend. The college butch. Each time the nest would unravel and, I, like a bowerbird, would look around, find someone new, and start building and rebuilding again. It was always a long winter, and then a long spring. Materials were never hard to find. Love, I thought, was all I needed to save me from myself. And then, as it all came hurtling down, I would realize again and again how wrong I had been.

6.

The moment I knew I needed to go to the psych ward was crystalline clear. Vespertine and I were on the precipice of breaking up. We planned to meet up to watch Paul Verhoeven's lesbian nun movie *Benedetta* and smoke weed and talk about how I felt betrayed, although when I arrived, we just had sex, rushed and dissociative and miserable. Then we watched the movie.

The following day I couldn't stop thinking about her: The date had been weird and strained and I knew the end was coming. To distract myself, I bundled up and went for a long walk in the Catholic cemetery two blocks away. I stopped in front of a gravestone with a faded pietà engraved on it, Mary's crying limestone face eroded into a cavernous-eyed alien grimace. Her mouth stretched wide as a frog's, and I took a selfie posing next to it, trying to make the same face. *Maybe I'll text this to her*, I thought, but never did. Instead, I went to a friend's for dinner and then went home.

I double-texted Vespertine that afternoon but got no response, despite her promise earlier that week to respond to my texts with more immediacy. This had been one of the things I asked for following our phone call. My head swam. It was 8 p.m. and I had no other plans so I ate a shriveled mushroom cap, savoring the mulchy taste on my tongue—not enough to fully trip, but enough to alter my mood into something more easily interpolative. I smoked an herbal cigarette as I waited for the shroom to kick in, but instead of feeling something—an ambient flowering, a fuzzy feeling rising within me—I just felt the same way I did before: like a girl alone at the bottom of a long well, the emptiness inside me infecting my surroundings, too.

My eyes started to water, and I refreshed my phone. No new messages. I forced myself to wait several more minutes before I refreshed again. No new messages. I already could tell I wouldn't be sleeping that night—shrooms gave me insomnia, even when they weren't working.

I took another drag off my cigarette and a spare ember floated down and singed an arm hair. It stung, but in a pleasant way, like the sharp relief of a smack on the ass from someone you loved. I took the cigarette out of my mouth and turned it around in the light of my desk lamp. It was several days after Christmas. I wasn't living with roommates, so I was completely alone.

Pain can be totalizing: If you're feeling it, you can't feel anything else. That's in part why my friends cut themselves, why I punched myself until it purpled. But I had been diagnosed with appendicitis months earlier and was waiting to get my appendix removed; if I hit myself there, I knew I'd have to rush to the emergency room. In the past several weeks, I had already run out of space around my tattoos to cut.

Something came over me, a mounting pressure I couldn't ignore. I looked down at the cigarette, the intoxicating orange bright at its tip. I looked at my reflection in the window above my writing desk. I looked at the arm where the ember fell—my right arm, my less dominant arm, a small patch of hair on it blackened slightly with singe. I thought about how much I wanted to stop the panic building in my chest. And then, as I pressed the lit cigarette against my skin seven, eight, nine times, I thought, *I need to break up with Vespertine* and *I need to get help* in simultaneity, over and over again.

The pain was first bright and then dull and then finally what I wanted, an intensity so vivid that I didn't think at all. I just felt, and as I started to weep, face mirroring the pietà, I knew I had crossed a line I would never be able to cross back from again.

I realized I couldn't be alone, so I made a schedule, texting friends to stay with, two a day, filling my time with others so I wouldn't fill it with hurting myself. This worked for about three days. On the fourth, drinking a Modelo winding through Prospect Park to my friend's apartment, my hand slipped, and the bottle shattered on the frozen soil. Glimmering in the moonlight, each thick glass shard on the ground called loud as a semitruck.

"I need help," I told my therapist the following day. "I can't make it stop."

After our session was over, at my request she started calling inpatient centers, finding one that would take my insurance. I called my mom, and she drove up. I texted Avery, still recovering from COVID, to let them know where I was going to be. And the following day, as snow started to fall onto the East River, my mother drove me to the psych ward, and then I was there.

In the psych ward, they took our clothes, but only for the first few days. During that time, we all wore long blue gowns and grippy colorful socks with toeholds on both sides, the same socks my father wore in the hospital as he lay dying. I could still shave under supervision and had access to my makeup, so I'd wake up, ask to lather, and then paint a deep scooped-out cat eye onto my face first thing each morning, before I even shuffled down the hallway for coffee. They gave me my T blockers in the same paper cup as the rest of my medication.

The ward, which my therapist found, was tiny, just twelve rooms wedged into a wing of a major university hospital. It was supposedly the least carceral place of its kind in New York City. Our windows looked out onto the old Bellevue, a sprawling shuttered complex in rusty brick and glass. We had one-on-one meetings with our psych team in the morning and group therapy twice a day, the second of which was led by an overly chipper WASP with an acoustic guitar who played Beatles songs and told us in a rehearsed up-pitch to "not worry about our problems!"

Some people were there to get better, but most of us were there to get out, and we found a sort of solidarity in our resistance to the bullshit: outdated references to brain chemistry, apolitical scripts we could say in response to bad bosses or toxic family members, intern visits. Because of the pandemic, the ward was more isolated than it had been in past years. It wasn't lonely, though. We couldn't eat meals together, so we made small talk passing each other in the hallway, wrote notes in one another's notebooks, played Monopoly together in the common area every early evening before curfew. The other people there saved me, and we complained about the same staffers together: the acoustic guitar bro, or the art therapist who would never tell us what time it was and encouraged us to "paint happy flowers," changing the subject whenever we asked questions about the length of our stay or her own history outside the institution.

My mom was in town, and she visited me several times, bringing takeout past the security guards and sitting next to me on my twin bed as I ate it, relieved to have a break from the same oversalted spinach or penne pasta that was served up every night. Avery, who started to pull away during the worst of my cutting, wrote an email every day wishing me well. I'd blush when people asked me about the outside. *I'm loved*, I would say, *I have people in my corner*. Vespertine and I were one week broken up and had stopped talking entirely.

There was solidarity with the other patients, and there were visiting hours, but there was also an abundance of unstructured time between the end of sessions in the afternoon and the dinner bell at 7:30. So when I wasn't with others, I spent most of my time reading, bringing used copies of Simone Weil's *Gravity and Grace* and Elissa Washuta's *White Magic* and Melissa Febos's *Abandon Me*. It was almost like an arts residency, but with stronger meds and worse food.

Before my admittance I had already started researching the micro-canon of women like me, those who had spiritual and emotional breakdowns because of white supremacy, capitalism, and their relationships. But I noticed none of these women were dating other crazy women, or at least they didn't frame it in that way: They were the abused and the other party was (rightly) the abuser, or they dated men who wielded their power over them in other ways, any symptoms of mental illness a function of their mistreatment. In Simone Weil's case, she wasn't seeing anyone at all, she just abjected herself before a God whose absence, to her, constituted presence. All of them, fundamentally, stood by themselves.

I'm tired of the argument that 1:1 representation—trans, partnered, whatever—is all that matters. Besides, I found myself in the writing of these women who were unlike me. I underlined each book with abandon and thought about Vespertine: every mention of love as a ferocious thing in Febos's collection; the sentence, "I couldn't write a book, because a book is the dénouement of a problem worked through in life" in Washuta's; Weil's unquenchable spiritual hunger, vivid as my own. But despite my recognition as I read, bright yellow socks on my feet, I still ached for something that represented the particularities of my life more specifically. I strived to see the sort of togetherness that hadn't shaped out yet in my life but maybe would, sharing a set of experiences with a lover who felt the same ways I did and building a life together anyway.

In *Antichrist*, Charlotte Gainsbourg's character loses her child. In the opening scene of the film, her son falls out the window as she and her therapist husband are having sex. And then, torn by grief, she loses her mind. Her husband, Willem Dafoe's character, begins treating her as his personal patient; they head to the forested cabin where she researched her dissertation, about violence against women. Soon, they both begin having visions in the woods; and shortly after, she begins torturing him.

After the death of her child, Charlotte Gainsbourg's character is consumed with the fear of being left; this, Willem Dafoe's character presumes, is why she becomes violent toward him. But he does leave her; he murders her, and he leaves her. The whole movie is essentially shot from his perspective, a narrative about a man discovering the evil his wife is capable of from the perspective of the man. But that just underscores its unreliability, one that is also emphasized by the husband's own visions, his own cocky abuse of patient-doctor boundaries; by the end of the movie, just like a medical professional, he pathologizes her, and leaves. She becomes just another dead, crazy, bad mother to him, and in this way, she was right all along.

To be crazy is to know your life has been marked as less than by those in positions of power; to date other crazy people is to assert your life's worth nonetheless. *Antichrist* is a comically misogynistic movie if you watch it from the man's perspective; it's a harrowing film if you watch it from the woman's.

This is why I'm devoted to growing through crazy for crazy relationships: Regardless of what else happens, parts of them remain and reflect back onto you. The bits and pieces of these relationships accumulate over time, and the intimacy they promise can reflect back into a greater intimacy with yourself. A hand intertwining with another on a couch. A text message apology, vowing to do better. The warmth blossoming when you see yourself in someone else, the representation I wish I had earlier in my life. Maybe if I knew what I wanted, could have seen it spelled out before, I would have made different decisions. My and others' deceit had eroded each relationship away, but the feelings, excavatable, remained.

When I was dating Vespertine, I dreamt of an essay that overflowed its borders and spilled into our real lives, whispering instructions on how to live as we whispered back. I saw a form that combined manifesto and confessional and the rough friction of one body's leg rubbing against another's, echoing into the small places between us and the damp chafe of underwear against jeans. When we dated (because she was also a writer), I wanted to write until my whole self purged and there was only the writing left, a writing so warm and present it reconstituted a self of its own. As we dated, I exhumed my misery again and again in the hope that it would fully flush the unhappiness out of my body and I could circle back around to joy, pulsing with a desire new to myself but enduring. When I thought about the future, I thought *not being sad* was the important part, rather than *staying alive*.

Then we broke up and I was left with the shattered forms of what I was trying to piece together. I thought I deserved what happened, blamed myself until there was nothing left to blame. Even now I confuse guilt and desire, slivering open the thick meat of each until only want is left.

Through and beyond pain, something else can grow, too. I believe this with the weight of my whole body. I have to. It's all we have.

7.

"I'm like a stray cat," I had said to my college partner once, trying to explain my own periodic absences and failures to text back, which were endemic. "I might leave, but I'll always come back."

But they misheard and started crying. "You're leaving?" they asked. Maybe they didn't mishear at all, and at that point just knew me better than I knew myself. I'd have almost the same conversation, on the opposite end, with Vespertine years later.

The most insidious belief we held at the boarding school was the illusion that we had no one else to turn to, that we were alone. And yet, we were all stacked on top of one another, the bathrooms I beat myself in sharing a narrow wall with the bedrooms next door. I'm sure my neighbors, also driven half-crazy by the school, heard me hitting myself late at night. I'm sure they saw through my attempts to hide my pain. I never acknowledged their presence, so I don't know how they would have responded to me. But there, we were never alone. We are never alone. When they wheeled me into the psych ward and the door closed with an antiseptic click, it felt like I was with all these people I loved again.

There's one more scene in *Antichrist* that still sticks with me. It's the last scene of the movie. Willem Dafoe's character has just murdered his wife. He pulls out the iron bar she hammered into his leg, lets the millstone bolted to it clank off onto the floor. Grabbing at counters and doorframes, dragging himself upward, he crawls out of the cabin they shared together, and finally he burns the body of the wife he murdered. As he climbs up a hill afterward, we see a bright light emerging, and then, dozens of women emerge, filling the frame completely. They climb up around him, too, hands luminescent, faces completely blank, emanating a blindingly present light. Willem Dafoe's character blinks as they ascend, and then the movie is over.

I've seen the women explained as victims of gynocide, too, coming for revenge against the therapist who murdered his wife. I believed that once, and if anyone asks me what the ending means, that's what I usually say. But that's not the reading I really prefer, the one I hold secret inside me. Instead, I think of the faceless women as part of the same shining constellation Charlotte Gainsbourg's character is—a host of women filled to the seams with a light too brilliant and complex for the world to contain, women lovable in their luminousness, stronger and even more capable than we could believe. I see a practice of care naked in its collective honesty. I see myself.

The last time I saw Vespertine, it was at a crowded book fair in Lower Manhattan. Our eyes briefly linked and then she looked away. It had been two months since I left the psych ward, but I didn't tell her that. We didn't talk, didn't approach each other. We raised eyebrows from across the room in surprise; we lingered; and we left.

I wound up spending ten days in the psych ward if you also count my time in the emergency room waiting to be admitted. I finished every book I brought, filled pages of my writing notebook, did the last passes of my essay on cutting for the magazine I pitched it for. And then I emerged, richer several new friends and a body blooming outward under the new medications I was taking, curves rounding my corners and filling my clothes. I felt at least conditionally at ease, the sort of ease you feel after going through an enormous thing and taking a long sleep afterward. I hated that psych ward, but I also found myself there. No. I hated the staff and the shape of the place, its long narrow hallway I walked down again and again. The other people confined there, I loved.

"The worst part of the story is the end," Elissa Washuta wrote in *White Magic*, and I underlined that part in the psych ward, too. But I don't think anything ends, not really. There's always a chance to get it right: if not with the same people, then with new ones, always a kind of optimism in knowing you can start again, hurt and be hurt less. Saving each other's lives is a way toward saving our own, too, although it's hard not to mistake one for the other.

Maybe how you love other crazy women is just: Carefully.

"No," I said while fucking recently, and the other person looked at me, and nodded thoughtfully, and said, "Okay," and then lay down beside me. That's a kind of love, too.

In the psych ward, I learned to grow more easy with silence; rather than throwing myself with abandon into relationships, I leaned into my own interiority as I started to reconnect with others. I had spent years avoiding naming myself as crazy, and then once I identified with it, I had a breakdown. But I was still learning to re-name myself even in the ward, still only beginning to learn how I could assume a fuller sense of agency again. In the ward, my roommate barely talked, and I stayed up far later than most of the other people there. So I'd walk from the rec room to my room, rec room to my room, hoping I'd bump into a friend but resigning myself to the quiet regardless, just like I was back in high school again. I loved myself, I realized as I walked. I was scared to be there, but not being there was even scarier. There was—after all—something I was afraid to lose. It was me.

When I finally got out, it was the third Monday of the year. Outside the building, I took off the surgical mask I had to wear the whole time I was there (even sleeping), and took in the deepest breath I could manage, body shaking with effort. The sun was still bright and high over Manhattan. The frost from that morning had just started to fade. I looked down the wide stretch of the East River, everything shimmering and blue, my mother waiting by the car. Standing outside of the building at last, it felt like finally coming into an ease with myself. It felt like a home slowly building itself back up. It felt like January.

Crazy love is tricky because it triggers me, but it also projects a future where we are held and cherished as well. Loving us, I realized, is the most direct route toward loving myself, too.

So I walked toward my mother in the driver's seat and we sped across the Manhattan Bridge, weaving through traffic into Flatbush. I stepped inside my apartment for the first time in almost two weeks, gingerly placing my hospital bag down on the hardwood, my life ahead of me all over again. My mother had been staying there, sleeping in my bed and watering my plants, and everything was slightly cleaner than I had left it, a promise toward the future.

As I crossed the threshold, I thought of everything I learned from my breakdowns, and what I'll learn from the ones yet to come. I thought of all of us crazy and in love, the knowledge and care collected between us, and the growth even through the pain we've shared. I thought of the life I've continued to build to this day. I think as we emerge into that future together, our very bodies will be glowing. I think at the end, arms linked, there will only be light.

Uncanny Valley of the Dolls

1.

The first time I learned about Greer Lankton, it was through a Facebook message from another trans woman. We'd met through a trans-specific arts scene in New York where everyone was hooking up with one another, a scene already notorious across the country; I had moved from North Carolina, in part, to be a part of it. The woman and I had been on several dates, but ultimately settled into a close friendship, trading DMs and texts and drinks with each other. A retrospective of Greer's life and work had opened and closed the year before I moved to New York, and during the year we were closest, before we started to drift apart, she sent me an article about it. The dolls Greer made—stunning, prickly, lovely—mirrored how I felt about my own body, alluring and off-putting in equal measure. It was 2017, four years after I had come out as trans and one year after I had started hormones. *When I first read about Greer*, my friend said in her message, *I cried*.

When I first started to transition myself, I was terrified of how rapidly my body was changing—breasts billowed out and body hair vanished seemingly overnight. So I learned to make myself beautiful to contain the fear, channeling it into presence instead. I comparison-shopped different brands of crimson and coral lipstick, drew my eyebrows on, taught myself to sway side to side to emphasize my gently swelling hips. And gradually, as I beautified myself (as I was *able* to beautify myself—beauty, like most things, follows racial and abled lines of power), things became easier. Less street harassment, more employment opportunities. I was quickly learning how I had to look to survive, and I resented that knowledge. Beauty, for me, became a shield, a way to dream a better world, a violence in what it granted me, all in simultaneity. In the article my friend had sent to me, the dolls appeared to struggle with that same burden, hungering under the sharp beam of others' perception. *Look at me*, they seemed to demand, their bodies rejecting or meeting those same gazes.

I love this, I messaged my friend back, and I started to cry as well. I had been working so hard at my own beauty that when I first saw a photo of Greer and her dolls, I was startled. The dolls glowed with a beauty I didn't even know I wanted until I saw it, after which there was nothing I wanted more.

2.

My favorite photo of Greer is in her bathtub. She is young, just twenty-six, and her blond bob is slightly wet, several strands tucked back behind her ears. Her shoulder bones stick out birdlike from her bare back, knees pressed tightly against her chest. She appears to be beaming, but there's a slight discomfort in her eyes, too. When I saw her the first time, I thought of my best friend from high school, Ashley, who had long, gorgeously unkempt hair and a similarly radiant smile. The past is always a hungry thing, tonguing at us until we reenter it. Who wouldn't think of it looking in the face of what was left behind?

In the photo, taken by Eric Kroll in 1984, she's cramped, confined to the lower sixth of the picture. The bathtub is full of suds. Around her, taking up the majority of the frame, are seven of the dolls she made: one doll gender-ambiguous with small sagging breasts and a penis protruding as if from a birth canal; two smaller dolls perched on the windowsill with pale, sticklike legs and small rosy nipples; a bald-headed, blue-lipsticked figure holding a small amber bottle in her lacquered hand—alcohol or maybe poppers; a fat doll, big breasts and a beautiful wide stomach circumscribed with a thick pink ribbon and frilly lace right below the bellybutton; and in the forefront of the picture, sitting on the tub in front of Greer, a massive doll at least seven feet tall—skin the color of undyed plaster and hair like a mass of electrical wire, red eyeshadow making two deep Vs underneath the cheeks, a bloody cross etched between the breasts that drips down red onto the corset compressing her chest below.

Greer's creations, like all dolls, are uncanny: They are like us, but not. In his 1913 essay "The Unfortunate Fate of Childhood Dolls," Rainer Maria Rilke wrote that a doll cannot be made into a person, or even a thing. Dolls, he notes circularly, are ultimately only dolls, fundamentally strangers to us humans. Greer, most known for the dolls she handcrafted from the late seventies through the early nineties, found companionship in that strangeness. She fashioned gossamer-thin eyelashes and eyebrows, gently curving fingers methodically painted lilac and periwinkle at their tips, expertly coiffed wigs set onto a head just several inches across. Sometimes they laughed haughtily, but mainly her dolls looked unhappy, leering, starved. Perhaps this is because Greer loved "severe beauty," bodies outside normative standards of gorgeousness: ones that are too much, excessive, too thin or too thick. She made dolls that looked like the bodies she loved. "I think when I'm making [my dolls]," she said, "something from me goes into them."

Unlike her dolls, Greer was conventionally attractive, pointed fawn-like features and light radiating from the wide toothy smile that occasionally broke across her face. While Greer's beauty could be intense, too (all high cheekbones and exposed ribs), it was a beauty she built herself, with a care that was as present in her being as it was in her dolls. She came out as trans at just twenty years old to what was, according to her diaries, a largely unsupportive world, and she found herself in her beauty, built whole theories around it. ("She could spend all day talking about beauty," her lifelong friend and sometimes lover David Newcomb told me.) But her work also suggests how being an object of desire could hold something more sinister, too. Her dolls—and her life—speak to the curdle of misrecognition caused by that beauty. To be beautiful means having access to what those not beautiful are refused: dates; money; attention, institutional and otherwise. But it can also mean not having anything besides beauty itself—confined to being the muse instead of the artist. Even Greer's thinness—linked to a lifelong, severe anorexia—was something taught to her by society at large: a box she ultimately couldn't escape, even if some of her dolls could.

But if the dolls refracted and challenged this gaze in ways Greer didn't always in her own life, they still functioned as objects of desire themselves. And the thing about being an object of desire is you have to deal with critics. Critic Marc Lida, in the *West Side Spirit*, called her exhibits "very disturbing"; Mary Thomas, in the *Pittsburgh Post-Gazette*, dubbed her last exhibition at the Mattress Factory "victim art"; Jan Avgikos, in *Artforum*, called her work in the Whitney Biennial "hideously glamorous." True, Greer's work unnerves, in that the dolls look alive, but not quite. Instead, they fall into the uncanny valley, a term the roboticist Masahiro Mori coined to describe the point at which a robot almost resembles a human but not quite. It derives from Freud's concept of the uncanny as a hidden thing once familiar, reemerged. To the transphobic viewer, we trans women fall into this gap. Our beauty, constructed against a society that fetishizes and hates us in simultaneity, is abject, and Greer's dolls are, too. They're gorgeous not in the way most women are but maybe in the way trans women are—a beauty shaped by and against societal expectations in equal measure. We love ourselves out of necessity when we're around others who don't. Greer herself explicitly linked her own beauty to her art. "Ever since I was little," she said in a 1984 interview, twelve years before her death, "I wanted to be a girl. It was an art piece deciding who I was going to be, the process of making myself pretty."

After she transitioned, Greer rarely referred to herself as a woman in interviews. She only *identifies* as a woman, she says at the 1994 Whitney Biennial, because "that's what I look like." What she looks like is gorgeous: tweezed eyebrows and heavily made-up face and kohl-lined eyes. Her dolls, too, resist fixed meanings or identifications, looking *like* instead of being something essential: Genitals shift regularly, and faces rearrange and are split and reconstructed and stitched together from the pieces of one another. As her work suggests, perhaps beauty is a dynamic action, one with the capacity to change. Perhaps beauty is what you do when you're told that you scare.

3.

Greer was born in Flint, Michigan, in 1958 to a Unitarian family. Her father, the pastor of the local church, announced her birth with a large IT'S A BOY on the church sign. She was a feminine child, tying a washcloth over her head into pigtails and "crav[ing] the glamour of a hairdo and lipstick." In a 1996 reflection on her early childhood, she notes, "I never was a flaming faggot . . . I was atomic." According to Greer, her parents' support was fickle and often wavered between encouragement and disapproval. This vexed relationship was only worsened by the profound betrayal she felt over their complicity in the childhood sexual abuse she suffered from age five onward at the hands of her maternal grandfather. From an early age, she failed to receive the protection she deserved.

But nevertheless, Greer endured—she'd light up the whole room with her presence, friends and family have said. From a young age, she developed art and movement practices, doing gymnastics, cheerleading, painting, and dollmaking throughout her preteen and teenage years. According to her childhood friend Joyce Randall Senechal, she made her first doll in middle school: a life-size teenage boy with long brown hair and a "stoned again" T-shirt, who might have looked like her at the time (she always wore her hair long). She built the doll out of old sewn-together T-shirts and acrylic paint, and this set a pattern: Greer would make dolls out of spare materials lying around, using wire coat hangers and soda bottles and torn-up umbrellas to make skeletons, building out musculature with clothes ripped into strips and adding in glass eyes to complete the look. "My doll obsession manifest[ed] itself at a very young age," she wrote when she was eighteen years old. "Dolls became more important than friends. . . . I feel my dolls in particular are very strong statements about 'the human condition'; by mirroring our exteriors they capture our souls."

Even before her hormonal transition, Greer had been living as a woman. At the 1976 alumni show at the Art Institute of Chicago, which she attended for a year after graduating high school early, Greer dressed up in a woman suit, a large doll she built and hollowed out inside, whom she called Madame Eadie: voluptuous, made from cloth, without genitalia. In the *Chicago Sun-Times*'s review of the show, Greer is misnamed and misgendered—the suit exceptionalized as the most lurid part of the opening, Greer's thinness and Eadie's fatness both emphasized to the press. Greer in the Eadie suit is described as someone who "who weighs 120 pounds but dressed up as a grotesque, overweight woman with her belly button hanging out"— the kind of derogatory language that will be used to characterize her work for the rest of her life. In her brief remarks to the *Sun-Times*, Greer insists that Eadie is fashionable, not grotesque—which I take as genuine despite her own intense anorexia and hatred of her body. The journalist, however, views this merely as a "claim."

It's not just her language; even how Greer moved in the suit shows how positively she felt about it. She continued wearing it into her college career, where—at times—she was shy, awkward, withdrawn. But "when Greer wore Madame Eadie," her Pratt friend Karen

Karuza told me, "she was the most confident and magnetic person in the room." There exists little public reflection from Greer on why she made her dolls, but perhaps they became a way for her to model a life before she lived it, a twinning that would continue through her whole career. Eadie's confidence—like that of Divine, one of Greer's idols—was aspirational for the woman she would become.

At nineteen, Greer had a mental breakdown after being assaulted at a bar, tried to kill herself, and checked herself into Riverside Hospital in Kankakee, Illinois. There, staff put her under an involuntary hold. She was institutionalized for more than two months—the first of several similar incidents in her life. According to case notes, the providers at Riverside focused on medicating and pathologizing her, rather than exploring why she might have been depressed. According to Greer, they may have placed too much emphasis on transness at the expense of the rest of her. Treatment notes from the following year describe a person with "strong feminine interests," but in later interviews, she characterized this period as filled with awkward feelings more than with explicit dysphoria. "I was never a man," she said, "but I was a boy." The hospital forced her sexuality and gender into binaries, telling her she had to choose between being gay and being a woman: She could not be both. Following her hospitalization and a brief period of "trying to be macho," as Randall Senechal described it, Greer got on hormones.

The following year, she went to see a surgeon in Youngstown, Ohio, for her vaginoplasty, but—owing to the flurry of mental health diagnoses she received during her psych ward stay and after—was rejected from several doctors she tried to see. She crowdfunded her surgery through her father's church—in a moment of greater support for her transition—and ultimately used the money to pay out of pocket for a less reputable surgeon who operated on the side, without medical oversight. Retrospectively, she expressed ambivalence about the surgery. She had felt rushed both by her parents and the medical establishment, which resulted in a subpar job. In a 1984 interview, Greer called this doctor's practice "the K-Mart of sex change operations."

After her surgery, Greer's career took off. By the time she was twenty-five, she had already appeared in group shows at the New Museum and PS1 and had also opened her first solo show at her friend Dean Savard's gallery Civilian Warfare in the East Village. "She pursues a deeper intimacy with human anguish and its multiform disguises than many older artists even dare to deal with, or experience," wrote the novelist and critic Gary Indiana after seeing this show. He went on to detail the dolls on display: a blood-drenched woman with a semi-erect penis birthing a group of "pepper-shaped" babies attached to a zippered egg sac (*Hermaphrodite*); a flat-chested, broad-shouldered gymnast bending backward to reveal her vagina, staring with blackened eyes at the audience between her legs (*Pussy Backbend*); a dark-haired boy in an athletic outfit with an erection springing out of his shorts into his hand (*Boy*). In the preoccupations of the show—childbirth, acrobatics, sexuality, the abject, despair—we see the preoccupations of her work and life.

That attention turned out to be fickle; it ebbed and flowed throughout her life. By the eighties, she was in the throes of a turbulent marriage with her husband, Paul Monroe, and her work—which she displayed publicly in the windows of his East Village boutique Einsteins—had seemingly fallen out of favor. Greer and Monroe separated in 1991, and, trying to detox, Greer moved to Chicago to be closer to her family. In 1993, she divorced Monroe; by then, the attention and critical profiles she received from institutions of record had vanished. (Monroe today runs a popular Instagram page dedicated to Greer's memory, linking his legacy to hers again; he presents himself as her devoted husband. He maintains that the divorce was a sham insisted upon by Greer's family.) There, she distanced herself from many of her friends, failing to connect with the people to whom she was once the closest, although she did gain new friends, like Chicago club kid and apprentice dollmaker Jojo Baby. She received some renewed attention in the last two years of her life, with invitations to be a part of the Whitney and Venice Biennials and her retrospective at the Mattress Factory, but after that Greer was dead. The papers that ignored her during her life wrote glowing obituaries.

In an interview with *i-D* in 1985, before she left New York, Greer was asked if her dolls "have problems." "Yes," she said. "Eating disorders, depression, they can't get jobs, their apartment's too small . . . all the normal problems all of us have. They stay up too late, smoke too much. They are not cute." It would be easy to read Greer's own troubles—drug addiction, romantic unfulfillment, sexual assault and family abuse, above all loneliness—as shaping the work that she made. She literally put herself in her art, after all: "Every time she sewed," Jojo Baby told me on the phone, "she'd accidentally cut her fingers, bleed inside the dolls."

But trans women's art is reduced to autobiography every day; our work, to outsiders, always reflects our own lives in 1:1 corollary. Invariably, everything we make is viewed through the lens of memoir, as opposed to something wholly original. Look at this book, for instance. Look at many of the books that historically have been published by us. For decades, the anecdotal evidence shows, autobiography was the only form of writing by trans women that major presses would publish and promote—even if many of those memoirs had more complicated aims beyond self-explanation. I refuse to confine Greer's own work to that narrow prism, too.

So, while Greer's work was admittedly an expression of her self, it was also more than that. She had a life outside of her dolls, and her dolls existed apart from her as well. Reading her work through the narrow keyhole of her pain eschews their complexity, the multitudes of moods, feelings, and characteristics they both contain and evoke: They're mischievous, scary, and seductive as well, in equal measure. It's easy to say that Greer's work was her life, but it's also simplistic. She lived beyond that, a life filled with the complexities of being an artist, an individual, and a trans woman. To remember her solely as a tragic figure, work yoked exclusively to her suffering, does a disservice to the life she lived. I love her work too much to do that.

4.

Greer had always been sick. She experienced excruciating pain her whole life, both from her vaginoplasty and from her hyperextended joints frequently sliding out of place. From childhood onward, she experienced intense asthma as well. The pain from all of this, goes one of the lines of thinking, was why she became an addict.

Ashley, my best friend in high school, kept repeating junior year because he was too sick to attend classes and our high-pressure residential school refused to give him a passing grade. Eventually he just withdrew. He never came out as trans but had long brown hair and a soft voice and he probably would have had he lived past eighteen. The last time I saw him before he left, he could barely get out of bed, so we just stayed in listening to Joanna Newsom off his MacBook speakers. He visited one time after he left, and I put him up on my double bed as I slept in a sleeping bag on the floor. That first day back, I snuck him into the cafeteria, us eating forkfuls of soggy spinach together and laughing at some stupid joke. Everyone I knew thought he was weird, but I thought he was beautiful.

By the end of her life, Greer could also barely get out of bed, although she drove herself to finish a blistering set of work deadlines anyway—two biennials and an installation at the Mattress Factory. Being trans and being sick for her were twinned experiences; at the start of college when Greer was still going stealth, Karuza told me, she had told her friends the hormone injections she needed to be driven to get were allergy shots to help with asthma. "Her favorite place was in hospitals," Newcomb said. "She felt safe there."

Ashley killed himself on New Year's Eve 2012. I know he killed himself because in the announcement of his death, which his parents logged in to his Facebook account to post, the cause of death was completely omitted. I know because he whispered to me once how hard things were for him, a sadness related to his disability but also deeper than that, somehow inarticulatable. He had reached out to me on Facebook Messenger several days before he died, asking me how I was, and I didn't respond until, unwittingly, after it happened. *Wishing you well*, he said. *I care about you.* And then he was gone, and never saw what I wrote back.

After he died, I couldn't bring myself to delete his number, so it kept transferring into new phone after new phone. The winter I eventually went to the psych ward I finally started texting him again. At first it was cautious. *Hey, Ashley*, I said. *Thinking of you.* Then, when no one replied, I sent a follow-up text. *I don't want to follow you*, I wrote. *I miss you so much.* Then, a week later, one last message—*I'm grateful for what we did have—sending you love.*

Within an hour, my phone lit up with a new notification. It was Ashley—or rather, it was the person who had Ashley's number, which had been reassigned sometime between my second and third text. *Please give me your name, sweetheart*, the person on the other end requested. I told them my middle name, the same as my mother's, and explained I was trying to text my dead friend. As I texted them, the bottle I had been holding in my hand slipped and shattered open in the park, almost like he had pushed me.

I'm so sorry for your loss and hope you will get past the hard time, they said, *I will pray for you Miss Rose.* And when I got that message,

I burst into tears and then checked myself into the psych ward a week later, mainly because it was the only way I knew at the time to not die and I wanted to not want to die.

If I love Greer Lankton's art, which I do, it's a love forged with every body I've seen laid down. It's a love fierce with how hard it is for us to stay living, how hard-won our beauty is. It's a love alive with the necessity of living, because not living would carve a hole in the other people you love. It's a love I have to believe she felt, too, until at the end, she didn't.

Scrolling through my phone's saved images when researching this essay, I passed the photos of my sister and my sister's things, the selfies of me with lovers or friends, until finally I came across a snapshot of my father on his deathbed. Lips parched and tube through his nose, he almost looked like a doll. It was 2017. We didn't know it was his deathbed when the photo was taken. I didn't even take the picture. My mother did, before I visited him, as if to say: This is what he looks like now. His skin, normally a flabby wine-purpled hue, was stretched tight and pale as parchment. His hospital gown dwarfed him. When I saw the picture again, it flung me back into the past, and I almost choked on the grief welling up even then.

5.

I suspect many other trans women have experienced awakenings similar to the one I did in response to Greer's work. I suspect this because so many other trans writers have written about her.

Over the past several years, there has been a renaissance in coverage about Greer following the digitization of her archives and the publication of her 1977 sketchbook, which she worked on during the year she decided to hormonally transition. Most of the reviews and essays written about her recently have been by trans women, and most of them, in turn, contextualize her within a larger ecosphere of trans women. Greer, the reviews emphasize, was like us, a sister lost to time.

This focus on Greer in terms of her connection to a trans community makes sense. Most of the cultural production about her in the decades prior—Monroe's memorial Instagram account; obituaries published after her death; several inches in *The New Yorker* and *Artnet* following her 2014 New York retrospective, the very exhibit my friend pointed me to in her initial Facebook message—had framed her as an artist existing by herself, absent of any community.

But Greer, both as an artist and a person, didn't stand alone, nor did she have a simplistically supportive relationship with other trans women, like the current writing about her suggests. In interview after interview, she separates herself from other trans women, demarcating firm boundaries. But she would also occasionally let them into her life. It was complicated. "I always love to meet transsexuals," she said, "but few are friends." Yet the relationships she did have are essential to understanding her life and work; the ambivalence she felt toward herself and to other trans women prevail in both.

In a 1992 letter to her friend Jan, Greer mentions one woman, Regan, whom she'd known for around fifteen years. Greer writes at length about how much Regan means to her: As "a transsexual recovering from heroin + cocaine," Regan had a lot in common with Greer, and for a time, the two were even lovers. "I love her so much," Greer wrote in the letter. Regan was dying of AIDS, and Greer believed there was nothing she could do to alleviate her friend's pain. Yet at the same time, she felt she had failed both her friend and herself. In the same letter to Jan, she notes that "My parents are proud of where I'm coming from, but I feel like I'm just surviving. Not that I don't have BRIGHT moments but it's hard and I'm lonely." And then a little later, in reference to either Regan or Jan: "I'm sorry I couldn't be a better friend." Regan—who Greer loved and felt she had failed—serves as a lens onto her relationship with her dolls, who were also often visibly trans.

There were other trans women Greer shared space with—notably the trans model Teri Toye, who she tried to pursue a friendship with in the '80s, when they both were still in New York. She was rebuffed. "If there are two of us together," Toye reportedly told her, "they'll gawk. That's what *they* want to see." Greer was crestfallen. But despite, or perhaps because of, these relationships, Greer rarely talked about other trans women to interviewers. She continued occasionally hooking up with other trans women, and exchanged letters with several more, but even those relationships were typically complicated. "I feel so much less of a woman with a woman," she once said.

In my own life, I found myself in relationships with other trans women—but we hurt each other, too. Vespertine, Siobhan, and so many others—it's impossible not to if you've been hurt yourself. The intimacy we found was frightening, true, but, unlike Greer, I still felt held and seen in these relationships, as complicated as they were. But maybe Greer felt similarly at times as well—because so few interviewers ever asked about her relationships with other trans women, it's difficult to ascertain the full extent of her feelings. Even preemptively, cisgender friends hesitated to associate her too closely with those like her. Greer's former roommate and friend Nan Goldin alludes to her—or society's—reticence when requesting to use her portrait in her 1993 book, *The Other Side*. Goldin writes:

"I'll only include you if you agree to it—I don't know how you'll feel to be in a book where the primary context is transsexuality + drag."

It's worth noting, though, that Greer said yes to Goldin's request after all.

More than supportiveness or disinterest, an ambivalence toward transness and trans peers is the most pronounced emotion running through Greer's work. Take a moving watercolor illustration, *Operation Day*, she made in 1981, where Greer dramatizes her vaginoplasty. It's a simple painting, almost cartoonish, the background flush with oceany blues and moss greens deep as a forest. Slashed across the frame is a pale body, pointy angles and sharp Egon Schiele breasts—presumably Greer's. Covering the bellybutton and forming a panty line around the legs are a series of medical-grade bandages, wrapped tightly, dappled pink with blood around the crotch. Through a hole in the bandaging, a catheter emerges, bright yellow urine running through it.

It's the text laid over the painting that's most striking: Written in pencil above and below her body are what appear to be memories of the surgery. "She feels a new fullness between her legs which seems to continue into her lower abdomen," Greer writes. "She aches without actually feeling." The text and illustration are both immensely tender, gesturing toward pain and becoming at the same time. It's unclear if the fullness she feels is good or not, which is part of the image's power. It doesn't assign a negative or positive value judgment. It just describes, as if in a state of light dissociation, the aftereffects of her surgery. The work presents transness without judgment *or* endorsement, a transness inseparable from the art itself, transness that reflects her relationship with other trans people, too.

I think about this watercolor when I see a later photograph of Greer, also in a hospital bed. Going off how soft her face is, I think she's probably in her mid-twenties, when she had surgery to deepen her navel. Her hospital gown is rolled up to reveal a series of bandages around her stomach where the operation happened. It's actually a doubled photograph, two pictures collaged on top of each other: a smaller Greer reclining on a larger Greer, her duplicated legwarmers touching each other. (I see this as a gesture toward complicated community, too: On one hand, there's not one trans woman there in the hospital bed with her, but two. On the other, they're both the same person.) She's smoking in the photos, looking off to the side. On the larger Greer's face, we see the beginnings of a smile. At the bottom corner of her hospital gown, a small brown bloodstain peeks out from beneath the folds. The stain would have been right around her midriff, but because the gown is pulled all the way up, it hovers, instead, right by her heart.

During my own recovery for surgery, my mother came with me. It was in Argentina in December 2023. My insurance refused to cover my facial feminization surgery, so, when I found out I had received an artists' grant from the state of New York, I used the money for a deposit and flew down south. During the two weeks we spent there, she took a polaroid of my face every day as it changed, eyes blackening and tissues swelling from the aftereffects of the surgeon's knife. I asked her to; I wanted a documentation of the procedure I could keep. I felt I was becoming more myself, and I wondered if Greer, who didn't have facial feminization but an array of other surgeries, ever felt like she was coming home to her own body during these procedures, too. I thought of her own practice of self-photography, the folders of pictures of her in the archive her parents assembled after her death.

Over our time in Argentina, I ate sweet tiramisu and lasagna from the restaurant down the street, and during the day my mother and I would watch more horror movies together, *La Llorona* and *Lake Mungo* and the television show *The Terror*, even though she hated being scared. She warmed to them over our stay. "I'm getting into these," she said after we finished *Picnic at Hanging Rock*, another movie about girls who can't love each other enough. "They're frightening, but there's a care to them, too."

As for me, I was building a more capacious beauty, and it scared me as well. The summer after my father died, I had a dream that the surgery, which I was considering at the time, made me hideous. The dream, like the one about my book, frightened me so much it took years to consider the possibility again. But in my apartment in

Buenos Aires, I realized it wasn't the new face that was scary, it was the anticipation of a future change. After all, what I made in the wake of my surgery was the most intoxicating thing I ever did. I made me.

Greer sought medical treatment frequently: in psych wards, rehabs, and above all hospitals. Being trans and being sick for her were twinned experiences. Even before her operation, her hyperextended joints often slid out of place, and her intense asthma had given her excruciating pain her whole life. As a result, she constructed both her life and her transness in relationship to the care she got.

This was a reason why her work and life spoke so much to me, too. My own joints bent at odd angles, and as a child I would nauseate friends by turning my hands around 180 degrees. "The Contortionist," Greer titled a short stop-motion film she made with Randall Senechal as a teenager, her body folding across a living room in hyper-sped-up motion. I found the film during my research, and for a day kept rewatching it. She moved similarly to me.

But we weren't the same, of course; Greer used her own disabilities as masks and interlocutors for her transness in ways I never embraced. According to Monroe, she would build her dolls in an operating theater of sorts, placing herself in the role of the doctor. Perhaps she imagined her dolls feeling as safe as she did when she worked on them. Perhaps her pain was shared by them as well, in its own process of creation, too. Perhaps for her, hurting was the only way she could think of being trans.

Throughout her life, the doll Greer worked on the most was the most like her. Greer started building Sissy in 1979 while recovering from vaginoplasty. Standing five-foot-eight and weighing 110 pounds, she had the same proportions as Greer herself. In some photos, Sissy stares out wearily, cigarette dangling from her lips; in others, her green eyes (the same shade as Greer's) are hooded and outlined in black, looking out vacantly. Sissy had a full set of teeth, which not all of Greer's dolls did, and great scooped-out cheekbones and a pronounced jaw. She made her public debut in 1982—fully naked and covered in jewelry, in the window of Einsteins. Greer placed a hand-lettered sign on a tray next to her that said, "Introducing— Sissy—you're welcome."

Sissy was a constant presence in Greer's life. Every time she learned a new technique in dollmaking, Jojo told me, Greer would rush to apply it to Sissy, too. I'd like to think that this was a gesture against loneliness, that Sissy served as a form of community to Greer. But also, in some ways, Greer's relationship with Sissy was fraught. She ripped her dolls open again and again to reform them, arguably its own kind of violence. And although she worked on her dolls while others were in the room with her, they seem to reflect the isolation she felt elsewhere in her life, too.

"Symbols always stand alone," the trans woman writer Kai Cheng Thom noted about her own relationship with community. During her life and posthumously, Greer has largely been perceived as a symbol—both as a source of aspiration for other trans women and as a tragic loner for the rest. This is part of the reason her work has received such renewed attention of late, the way her actual self was stripped to create someone we could project our own selves onto. Relegated to merely a symbol, Greer's actual relationships to both dolls and trans women are glossed over.

One way to think about community, which Greer couldn't fully access in her lifetime, is as a resistance to this oversimplified fame. But our lives, if we long for fame—and of course trans women do; being famous is one of the deepest dreams of those for whom every safety net has been taken away—are concurrent with attempts, self-imposed and external, to silo us away from others like us. To be famous is to be accepted en masse when you haven't been accepted before; and to be famous is to be alone. Greer's work speaks to the loneliness, violence, and isolation inherent in that pursuit of fame, while also pointing to the messy, at times disappointing bonds she formed with other trans women, too.

In Buenos Aires, my mother went out to get food for me every day, and other trans women—my friends and my girlfriend, whom I had been seeing at that point for just three months—called regularly. I woke up to text messages checking in on me and started talking on the phone when I was recovered enough to do so. Blinded by the flash of the Polaroid camera every day, unable to sleep lying down, face swollen, I couldn't do anything, really, but watch movies. But in the constant check-ins and the space the surgery afforded me to rest, I realized I had built the kind of life I had dreamed of for years, the life I moved to New York initially for—one filled with love and care and community. I had stayed alive, and the people in my life were grateful for my life.

That wasn't fully the case for Greer at the end. Before she died, she stripped Sissy to reskin her, changing the doll from her likeness to that of a lover's, perhaps (according to Jojo) another trans woman. As she disassembled the doll, the blank face underneath the face emerged; then its spindly skeleton. And it remained like that for a long time. She didn't get to reassemble the doll before she died, so it hung off a coat hook in the closet of her parents' house for years. Where the heart should be, she had painted the same phrase in red ink that went inside every one of her dolls, clear as the brown on her hospital gown or the pink between her legs in *Operation Day* or the neatly inked lines in her letter about Regan.

"Love me," it said.

6.

The girls tend to die early. Mainly suicide, if we're talking about the white ones; suicide and murder if we're talking about the non-white ones. Every trans woman I know has a story about the late-night phone call, the sudden disappearance, the (as writer Torrey Peters frames it) funeral as social event. Being trans, especially being a trans woman, is hard: systemic discrimination and prejudice, medicalized gatekeeping, the constant hovering threat of violence from lovers and onlookers. It's harder the more intersecting oppressed identities you have. Killing yourself in a world that wants you dead is a capitulation but one hard to resist.

Greer died at home on November 18, 1996. She was alone, without her family or friends. She had just completed a retrospective for the Mattress Factory, wherein her home had been moved to the museum to be preserved. According to the toxicology report, Greer died of a cocaine overdose; she had started using again to meet the deadlines of her last few shows. According to a letter they wrote to notify friends and family of her death, her parents, who found the body, weren't surprised. In their letter, they memorialized their daughter's life, using language at once caring, honest, and dismissive.

> *Our daughter led a parallel life. She had a bright, creative side. . . . She also had a dark, destructive side (including drugs, an attraction to the "underside" of society, & abuse of her body). From the first year of life, Lynn thought her journey through life would be "different." She was born a boy but at 21 she had an operation and became a woman. This never completely healed her difficulties. . . . We supported her emotionally and financially right to the very end.*

Crossed out in the middle of the typewritten paragraph in which they describe her life, they write, "Things could not have gone better."

While Greer's death was ruled an accidental overdose, her illness and previous history of suicidality cast a long shadow over whatever happened. As a teenager, Greer had checked herself into Riverside because of these impulses, which were also almost certainly related to her sexual trauma. Throughout her life, there had been multiple attempts at taking her own life: one intentional overdose and several accidental ones, in addition to many hospitalizations, both voluntary and involuntary.

If you're looking for it, suicide is everywhere in her work. Sissy, hanging in the closet. Various dolls' emaciated frames morphing into omens of death. According to her notes for graduate school applications in the mid-1980s, even the seven-foot doll posing in her bathtub with a cross carved into the chest was a reference to suicide. A relative of Greer's had attempted to kill herself in the exact same way years earlier.

The fact that Greer was so frequently suicidal is an indictment of the world she lived in—her "difficulties" were not innate but imposed upon her. But the fact that Greer continued to live after this first attempt is a testimony to her endurance in the face of hardship nonetheless. I know for myself, learning to live was the most important thing I've ever done, and the hardest. Through doing so, I had to reject what I was taught about the kind of life available to me. And despite the proliferation of deathly art she made, according to her diaries and friends, Greer lived fully, too.

Again and again, throughout my interviews, loved ones would emphasize how funny Greer was when she was alive, how much they loved talking with her. "She'd hold court," Karuza told me. For those who survived her, these remembered conversations are just as important to her memory as her art. "Her work was her form of communication," Goldin said in a promotional quote for Greer's last show, but if it was, it's a one-sided communication: The dolls can't listen or respond to their audience. Only Greer could do that. Her legacy can never fully encompass who she was. An archive is never a replacement for a person themselves. "She taught me how to make dolls," Jojo Baby told me when we talked on the phone. "I've kept making them because that's the only way I can still hear her talking to me."

"I am haunted," Thom writes. "All trans women are. Behind me stretches a line of ghosts—trans women, killed before their time by the hatred of a society that does not know how to love us.... Perhaps this is why trans women dream so deeply—because we walk hand in hand with those in the next world." No one was with Greer when she died, so it's impossible to know if her death was a suicide or an accident or the result of overwork and neglect. However, the distinctions between those categories (I believe) are blurrier than most would maintain: all point back to the systems that kept her ill. Regardless of what happened, her art reflects a trans woman who tried several times to die but made beautiful things, who had an unfillable emptiness that she tried to fill nonetheless. And even though it's a poor substitute for her still being here, the work remains as powerful as it was when she was alive. Her art has lasted because it walks in that next world, too.

Dolls is also a slang word for other trans women, an irony present in the many profiles written about Greer that compared her to her creations. True, she posed herself doll-like in pictures throughout her career—including in an ad for her Civilian Warfare show where she stretched out, fully naked, surrounded by her dolls—but more than that, Greer was a doll herself: a doll who made dolls, a doll surrounded by dolls, a doll alive in ways her creations weren't. Even if she looked dead in earlier photos, she wasn't.

Depicting death can also be a way of accessing life, though I don't know if Greer believed that. I know when I was most suicidal, I dreamed of making a flipbook cataloging every single way I could die: wrists slit, head gored open, pancaked jumping off a tall building. By writing it all down, I thought I could get those urges out of me, choosing life instead of its absence. But I was too scared to actually commit to the project. Drawing these deaths, I feared, would make them more real. Greer's dolls, in contrast to my imaginary sketchbook, are real. They—pale-skinned, bony-limbed—live on after her death still.

I can't speak to her motives or thoughts, although when my own suicidality was at its most intense, it was driven by an unalterable sense of loneliness, a sense that my own existence was a punishment, a mistake. I harbored a bitterness that felt inescapable, that I know, from so many late-night phone calls, that other trans women possess as well: feeling as though the world has foreclosed on your life—because in many ways, it already has.

It's perhaps hackneyed to say, but what saved me was the love of others like me, embracing the messiness and care present in our lives and work. And this complex negotiation echoes what I see in Greer, too. I, too, have struggled to live. I, too, have struggled to love myself and other trans people. I, too, have realized that loving yourself isn't a panacea for a world that doesn't love you. At various times, I've felt an urgency to live and a simultaneous urge to die. In Greer's work are those same tensions. I finally realized: I've been drawn to Greer's work for all these years because in it, I see a world I've walked in as well.

7.

When she was in treatment for drug abuse in the 1990s, Greer made a list of her strengths, jotting them down in red Sharpie. There are twenty-eight items, ranging from "compassionate" to "survivor" to "street smart" to "risk taker" and everything in between. "Love to learn," one of them says. And toward the end of the list, an entry that is partially scratched out, as if she wanted to say something, stopped herself, and then said it anyway: "wants to be healthy."

Greer struggled with depression, drug abuse, and anorexia her whole life. ("Anything over three digits is a danger zone," she once painted on her bathroom scale.) By the end of her life, she was incessantly calling friends for money, deep in the throes of addiction, and gradually they stopped seeing her because of this. But in her diaries and photos from before the end she had moments of pleasure, too, however brief. A set of notes on a night out on the town, a picture of her beaming next to another trans woman at the Biennial, a small heart drawn in her diaries next to the name of a man she just had sex with—all are evidence of the happiness and companionship she felt with others, too. "I will not die," she wrote in her 1977 journals, shortly before deciding to transition. "I will become." On the following page is a drawing of her own silhouette, garish eyeshadow and a sneer on her face. In the drawing, she looks tough and fierce, and she looks beautiful.

All told, Greer made at least three hundred dolls during her life—not including the dolls she remade. Her work is scattered among various individuals and institutions—between private collectors, Monroe Jojo Baby, David Newcomb, MoMA, and the Mattress Factory, among others. And in this collection—photographs, dolls, journals, and other documentation—the shadow of her life remains. Greer posing next to a doll, face heavily lined and crumpled at thirty-six. Greer ten years younger, staring down the camera over a smoldering cigarette. Greer at twenty, in her freshman year at Pratt, laughing at a joke told by her dormmate who snapped the photo. Greer's face sparks with joy, at least for a moment.

"Greer's work was like surgery without anesthesia," Goldin wrote in the *New York Times* memorial. "Her work came out of her need to create art to survive, and it took tremendous courage to reveal herself to such an extent." But survival wasn't only in her art; it was at the root of her life as well.

When Greer was fourteen, she had a tooth extracted, and she drew a comic about it afterward. The drawing, done in pencil, is far more lighthearted than the work she would become famous for, but even then, a melancholy still courses through it. It depicts a bizarre birthing scene, in which a series of "old teeth," smiling in a line next to each other, are nestled into a set of gums. One tooth, blackened with cavity and wearing an expression of resignation, is being yanked out with a set of pliers. "Old tooth being taken up to the big heavenly denture in the sky," reads the caption.

At the bottom of the image is a small human, "a little man whose job is to push the new teeth forward to a new life." Arms fully outstretched, he pushes a baby tooth out through the gumline. The teeth are smiling because they're happy for someone new to arrive. "Welcome," the tooth with the biggest smile says. In the drawing, we see early glimpses of a theme that will pervade her work for the rest of her life: a world where vulnerable things are safe, where they endure. Birth is welcomed, and death doesn't hurt. I really hope Greer believed this, too. I hope every one of us dolls continues living.

It's easy to have community with ghosts, because they're everywhere. It wasn't just Ashley, or me: Chrissy was self-destructive, too. Like Greer she spent time in clinics and died before her time, leaving behind an archive, a smaller one, that my mother grievingly pulled together. I don't know what my sister's death was like, but I know the feeling of making yourself out of the impossibility of someone who used to be there. Sometimes I wonder if we just reenact the same life patterns of those who haunt us, but if we do that reenactment is surely a two-way street: If grief is an act of love, then leaving a ghost of yourself behind is as well. Sharing an experience with someone who isn't there anymore, I have to believe, is a way of communicating with them, too.

After I got out of the psych ward in 2022, I checked my phone and that picture of Greer in the bathtub—blond hair swept like she usually wore it behind her ears, grinning wide with all her teeth in the flash of the camera—beamed backed at me. On and off, it had been my phone background since 2017. And in that photograph and others, surrounded by the things she made, Greer remains—a ghost, a girl, someone who was and still is remembered to this day.

Then, a text from my mom, obscuring the image.

"I'm here," she said, "I'm so glad you're alive."

Postlude

At the writing residency I attend six months after the psych ward, we get our own rooms with doors that close and mirrors loosely fixed to the walls. The air is nippy, much cooler than in Brooklyn. I haven't packed the right clothes at all, so I walk around shivering in borrowed sweaters, black denim short-shorts poking out underneath. There's a gentle mist settling over the property like in an old werewolf movie, wild thyme growing in thick thatches across the ground. Each morning, I wake up early—far earlier than I do in the city—and make myself toast and a vegan omelet; each morning, I breathe in the cold sting of the air as I step outside with my breakfast; and each morning, I still can't stop thinking about you.

For me, horror is a love language, but maybe that's because for me everything is a love language. Horror at its most intimate is a way to share the secret parts of yourself with others: what frightens you, what comforts you, what you're nonplussed by. At the start of so many relationships I've cared about, we couldn't relate to each other, and we smoothed that distance over with horror movies humming in the background: fucking instead of talking after Halloween parties or holding hands through New Year's Eve confessions that still didn't reveal everything. We substituted the things in our life that scared us for things on a screen. And by the time these relationships finally ended, we barely knew the difference between the two.

If you watch enough scary things, gradually what scares you shrinks; you become tougher, more inoculated to it. But even if the feeling goes away, the root of that fear remains. At the residency, I stay in a cabin much like the one in *Antichrist*: rustic and rutted with trees nearby. There, I write page after page of notes; I hike up and down a trail bursting onto a cliffside overflowing with bark and birch; I rewatch *Ginger Snaps*—blood and sex and bristly fur, one of the first movies we saw together; and I don't talk to you. I can't. Like a scene from a horror movie, there's no cell service, so my texts go undelivered. It's only when I return to the city that we'll, at last, break up for good.

To be scared in the presence of someone else is to open yourself to vulnerability. We watched movies together and we loved each other and it hurt, but being wounded isn't enough reason to stay in something that continues to wound.

I'm only realizing this now, as I write it. You can't unpack what you're afraid of when you're still feeling that fear. Emotions are the only thing you can access. According to a 2017 study, patients with PTSD (again, that troublesome term) experience hypervigilance and reduced cognitive processing when shown "unpleasant images." The study frames this response as a sign of damage, but I see it as a state of overwhelm that can be productive, too. Horror, after all, is foremost an exercise in feeling things—a way to access states of emotion otherwise foreclosed. Horror can be a way to feel closer with others feeling the same thing—a way to discover yourself as well.

In *The Texas Chain Saw Massacre*, there's a moment at the end of the film when the protagonist, Sally Hardesty, escapes the villains. Sally's on the back of a flatbed, speeding away. Leatherface has just sawed through his leg and limps around, chainsaw raised. "Drive faster!" Sally yells, and then, wide-eyed, she starts to laugh—a harsh laugh, full of fear choking down her throat.

I want people to be more than the sum of what's done to us, but sometimes I'm scared that the trauma just shovels into our skin anyway, hollowing us out from the inside. Rewatching *Chain Saw* the summer before the pandemic starts, this fear activates again all of a sudden: That I'm just like Sally. That if I push further or go through anything else I'd go mad, hurtling toward a full breakdown. That my life is linear, and if I hit that one nadir, the amount of life left afterward will simply run out.

Sally has seen everyone she loves cut to pieces or stuffed in a frozen locker like meat. When she laughs at what's happened, it's a laugh without relief, a laugh that takes her over completely. And when the movie cuts to credits, Leatherface swinging his big chainsaw to the camera, she's still laughing.

When I was a child, my greatest fear was losing who I was through what happened to me. And yes, I've lost myself again and again. But in the wake of the violence that shapes us, I've also found myself more fully than I ever could have without the wound. Sure, in *The Ring*, *Dark Water*, and countless other films, an uncanny return from what seeks to kill you is one of the greatest horrors the filmmakers could imagine. Samara, rising from the well water. Yoshimi, realizing, as she ascends to the roof, that she's holding a ghost child in her arms, not her own flesh and blood. Even in *Scream*, Sidney's own grief animates everything that comes next—up until the end of the movie, when she limps out of the house after stabbing her boyfriend and would-be murderer, surrounded at last by friends hurt in similar ways as she herself has been.

Scary movies are scary because they show us versions of ourselves we don't want to see: ones crueler or more ragged with trauma. They tell us that what happens to us is irreversible, our lives a sunset occurring once and never again. They tell us a person can only go so far until they snap. But humans aren't frozen rubber bands, stretchable to only a certain point before we break; nor are we unstoppable monsters, hurting everything around us until we're dead. We're blood and bone, and the things we've endured are committed by people who are those things, too.

That, maybe, is what makes it scary. Not a man with a chainsaw or a dripping girl in a well, but the fact that we can hurt others without even meaning to. The pain we can cause, and the legacies left behind by that pain anyway.

If horror is a sign of love, it's one marked by love's impossibility. Even the horror films with happy endings aren't happy, really; their protagonists still roil open from what's happened to them. On the drive back from the psych ward, I knew I wasn't "fixed"; I refuse that language. But I knew a life I could live and love within was visible again.

It's late afternoon, the sun a shock of vermilion against the lake. Even though it's almost dinnertime, I still have just enough time for a walk up the lakeshore. When I arrive at its expanse, the water is cool and crisp, dark gray and streaked with sunset. The grass by the water's edge tickles the soles of my feet as I pull them out and the dinner bell resonates from the clubhouse, a deep clang. As a child I fantasized about moments like this—the evening air, more temperate than down south, pricking at my skin; work done for the day, alone in the moment but decidedly not uncared-for. Then, I dreamed that the problems I faced would disappear. As I pull on my shoes and start to hike back to the house, lemony spurts of thyme air up with every step I take. It lingers in my lungs even here, up north.

Here's how things will progress, my last breakup before I start writing this book. When I get home, we'll put on a movie in the background, make sure the couch is flush with pillows for your back and braces for my wrists. We'll break up and we'll both cry, but we'll continue to grow. We'll hold the fear.

On one of our first dates, you press me against the hard stone of a Prospect Park bridge, night glinting with moon and fog. Later, in the same monochrome haze, you hold me tight as we watch *Black Swan*. Or you were my friend's roommate and told good stories and had long eyelashes and soft lips, your voice bright as a lake. You leave New York, and we watch movies with each other over Zoom, violent films crafting another bridge even as we lived a country width apart. Or you come over to watch *Antichrist*, and I won't even realize it was a date until after you leave. Charlotte Gainsbourg's face fills the screen in her only moment of pleasure before her whole world falls apart, and we don't know yet that ours will, too.

Or it's summer 2023, a year after the writing residency and a year and a half after the ward. We've just met at a party in Oakland to commemorate a friend's surgery. You're funny and smart, with gorgeous cheekbones and loose curls and good questions, and a month and a half later, you will come to stay with me in New York for a music festival that sells out before you could buy tickets. So instead, for our thirteen-day-long first date, we go out dancing in the city to all the clubs we can get into for free and traipse through museums and watch a different scary movie every time we see each other afterward, traveling across the whole country every few months as we fall further and further in love with each other: *Pearl* and *Audition* (again) and *Crimes of the Future* and *Phase IV* and *Chain Saw* (again), our hands and bodies tighter against each other with each film. It's now summer 2024 and the whole household is sick, COVID tests stacked on your bedroom table just in case, and you're still sitting next to me in your bedroom right now, mask on, as I write these words. It's still you.

I think of those first dates, girls or former girls uncanny in the light of our love—and although I don't know what precisely will come, I think of the future as well. Across the lake of the residency, a wood creature lows. Night is finally settling in, and I'll have to pull on a sweater soon. Maybe you're pulling on thicker clothes, also, whoever or wherever you are.

Being in the present—which is to say, presence—implies a future, too; caring in that moment shapes that future. Presence makes a path to find future presence, too. It shows us a life, struggles linked in love and fear alike. Like a final girl, a sick girl, a girl in the well, I know I won't heal from what I've done or what was done to me. But I'm not interested in being healed nor in my wounds being reopened: What I want now is to love the scars that make us us.

A flash of blood transforming into hope. A girl turning into a wolf. A host of faceless women all marching up a hill. As I enter the clubhouse for dinner, I'll only hear the unsteady metronome of the present—unknown, unwinding, scary, and free. Fear has a thumping rhythm to it, but so does being present with people you care about, and that's what I choose to listen to now. I'll walk to the dining table, the thuddy sound of love rumbling underneath everything like a heater slowly clanking up to speed. Even if the French psychoanalysts are right and horror *is* about the rotten, the dead, the makeup-less, the sick; even if we're confined to the abject, the unwell, the uncanny—that's beautiful, too. Yes, I've lost myself through the things that have happened to me, but so have you. So I'll sit down at the table with my new friends, far away from you, and you, and the you I haven't met yet, and fix my plate and fill my belly, eating to satiation at last.

Soon it will be completely dark outside and the coresidents will start trickling to bed. I'll wash my plate, and while the other writers and artists start their nighttime routines, I'll start my own: I'll walk down by the lake again, dip my feet into the water, and think of the present to come. My legs, still healing, will throb from the exertion of walking down the hill, but that's part of what being present means: accepting pain as a prerequisite for being alive.

The feeling will surge into me like a movie starting to spool, and, not for the last time, I'll start to cry. As I sit there, a loon will call, and then, from the far side of the lake, coyotes. Inside my head, though, the only sound left will be that of my, and your, future: its immediate, encompassing noise. How beautiful, how frightening in its pitch. It sounds like our home. Even now, I hope you hear it, too.

Acknowledgments

This book would not exist without the host of readers, friends, and loved ones who read drafts or were cornered by me at a party as I talked endlessly about horror movies: Lea Anderson, John Manuel Arias, Kay Ulanday Barrett, Sol Brager, Catching On Thieves, V Conaty, S. Brook Corfman, Madeline ffitch, T Fleischmann, Sloane Holzer, Joselia Rebekah Hughes, Rax King, Jess Lempit, Chris Littlewood, Kyle Carrero Lopez, Benedict Nguyen, Soraya Palmer, Dema Paxton-Fofang, Río Sofia, Mimi Storm, Siobhan Viles, Harron Walker, Lu Yim. Additional insights in this book came from conversations with every ex and partner named or unnamed, in addition to everyone I've ever watched a creepy movie with.

Thank you so much to my brilliant and fastidious agent, Amy Bishop-Wycisk. This book would not exist in the world without all your work.

Thank you, too, to my incredible editor, Ezra Kupor, who made this work so much stronger, more intellectually rigorous, and more curious and compassionate about the world it exists in. And the rest of the Harper team, too: my copy editor, Kim Daly; my cover designer, Caroline Johnson, and book designer, Jen Overstreet, who both captured the look of the book so precisely; my marketer, Daniel Duval; and my publicist, Nicole Sklitsis.

Thank you so much to Julia Armfield, Johanna Hedva, Rax King, Elissa Washuta, Carmen Maria Machado, Torrey Peters, and Jeanne Thornton for their kind words and support.

Thank you, as well, to the publications and projects that published earlier versions of these essays: *The Believer, The Offing, It Came from the Closet* (Feminist Press, 2022), *Electric Literature*, *Catapult*, *Bright Wall/Dark Room*.

Willow Catelyn Maclay writing on *Ginger Snaps*—first on her Patreon, and then in her book with Caden Mark Gardner, *Corpses, Fools and Monsters: The History and Future of Transness in Cinema* (Repeater Books 2024) first drew my attention to some of the trans elements of the film. Moreover, the Greer Lankton chapter would not exist without the diligent and generous work of Sarah Hallett, the senior archivist at the Mattress Factory, nor without S. Brook Corfman's and Grace Byron's own scholarship and reportage on her.

So much of this book was written and conceptualized in residency at Blue Mountain Center, which helped me conceptualize one way a writing life looks. I'm indebted to my full cohort, some of whom are named above, in addition to the staff who made the space possible—especially Romy Felder. Thank you for *Waiting for God*.

Thank you so much to my mother, who first taught me grace.

And thank you to every ex and partner I shared and share a life with. It's been transformative, a thing of beauty, in more ways than I can name.

Sensitive or Triggering Subject Matter

The list below, organized chapter by chapter, attempts to catalog the most common areas of potential trigger. Take care of yourself as you read.

Prelude—self-harm, psychiatric confinement

The Girl, the Well, the Ring—grief, medical neglect, transmisogyny

Our Oceans, Ourselves—murder, drowning, colonialism, anti-Blackness, sexual assault, anti-Indigenous violence and dispossession

Ghost Face—anti-Blackness, anti-Indigenous violence and dispossession, murder by police

War on Terror—war crimes, torture, Islamophobia, child sexual abuse, physical assault

Southern Fried—self-harm

Cutting in Miniature—grief, murder, alcoholism, transmisogyny, self-harm

Preliminary Materials for a Theory of the Werewolf Girl—sexual assault, transmisogyny

Devotion—grief, car crashes, eating disorders, transmisogyny

Crazy in Love—psychiatric confinement, self-harm, sexual assault, murder, suicidal ideation

Uncanny Valley of the Dolls—transmisogyny, child sexual abuse, eating disorders, psychiatric confinement, attempted murder, addiction, suicide and suicidal ideation

References

Prelude

"Box Office History for Horror." *The Numbers.* https://www.the-numbers.com/market/genre/horror.

Kristeva, Julia. *Powers of Horror: An Essay on Abjection.* Trans. Leon S. Roudiez. Columbia University Press, 1982.

The Girl, the Well, the Ring

Pet Sematary. Directed by Mary Lambert, written by Stephen King. Paramount Pictures, 1989.

Piepzna-Samarasinha, Leah Lakshmi. *Care Work.* Arsenal Pulp Press, 2018.

Ring, The. Directed by Gore Verbinski, written by Ehren Kruger. Dreamworks Pictures, 2002.

Your Swan, My Swan

Black Swan. Directed by Darren Aronofsky, written by John McLaughlin, Andres Heinz, and Mark Heyman. Fox Searchlight Pictures, 2010.

Our Oceans, Ourselves

Dark Water. Directed by Hideo Nakata, written by Yoshihiro Nakamura and Kenichi Suzuki. Toho, 2002.

Dark Water. Directed by Walter Salles, written by Rafael Yglesias. Touchstone Pictures, 2005.

"Elizabeth City Township, Pasquotank County, North Carolina." United States Census Bureau. https://data.census.gov/profile/Elizabeth_City_township,_Pasquotank_County,_North_Carolina. Accessed July 31, 2024.

Enjeti, Anjali. "The Haunting of Lake Lanier." *Oxford American* 113 (2021). https://oxfordamerican.org/magazine/issue-113-summer-2021/the-haunting-of-lake-lanier.

Kincaid, Jamaica. *A Small Place*. Farrar, Straus and Giroux, 2000.

Ringu. Directed by Hideo Nakata, written by Hiroshi Takahashi. Toho, 1999.

Simpson, Bland. *The Mystery of Beautiful Nell Cropsey: A Nonfiction Novel*. University of North Carolina Press, 1993.

Tipton, Michael and Hugh Montgomery. "The Experience of Drowning." *Medico-Legal Journal* 90, no. 1 (2022).

Tuck, Eve and C. Ree. "A Glossary of Haunting." *Handbook of Autoethnography*, ed. Stacy Linn Holman Jones, Tony E. Adams, and Carolyn Ellis. Left Coast Press, 2013.

Ghost Face

"'A Warrant Is Not a License to Kill': Rev. William Barber Condemns Police 'Execution' of Andrew Brown." *Democracy Now*, April 27, 2021. https://www.democracynow.org/2021/4/27/andrew_brown_jr_police_killing.

"Above the Law? Review of Police Killing of Andrew Brown Jr. Demanded After DA Calls It Justified." *Democracy Now*, May 21, 2021. https://www.democracynow.org/2021/5/21/andrew_brown_jr_police_killing.

Couch, Aaron. "Melissa Barerra Dropped from *Scream VII* After Social Media Posts Concerning Israel-Hamas War." *The Hollywood Reporter*, November 21, 2023. https://www.hollywoodreporter.com/movies/movie-news/melissa-barrera-fired-scream-vii-1235669458/.

"Lack of Diversity in U.S. Coast Guard Greater in Higher Ranks; Comprehensive and Sustained Changes Recommended to Improve." RAND, August 11, 2021. https://www.rand.org/news/press/2021/08/11.html.

Sayers, Daniel O. *A Desolate Place for a Defiant People: The Archaeology of Maroons, Indigenous Americans, and Enslaved Laborers in the Great Dismal Swamp*. University Press of Florida, 2014.

Scream. Directed by Wes Craven, written by Kevin Williamson. Dimension Films, 1996.

Scream 2. Directed by Wes Craven, written by Kevin Williamson. Dimension Films, 1997.

White, Adam. "Kevin Williamson: 'The Scream Movies Are Coded in Gay Survival.'" *The Independent*, December 6, 2021. https://www.independent.co.uk/arts-entertainment/films/features/kevin-williamson-scream-interview-b1968631.html.

War on Terror

Center for Substance Abuse Treatment (US). "Exhibit 1.3–4, DSM-5 Diagnostic Criteria for PTSD." *Trauma-Informed Care in Behavioral Health Services* (Treatment Improvement Protocol (TIP) Series, No. 57), 2014. https://www.ncbi.nlm.nih.gov/books/NBK207191/box/part1_ch3.box16/.

Crocq, Marc-Antoine and Louis Crocq. "From Shell Shock and War Neurosis to Posttraumatic Stress Disorder: A History of Psychotraumatology." *Dialogues in Clinical Neuroscience* 21, no. 1 (2000): 47–55.

Edelstein, David. "Now Playing at Your Local Multiplex: Torture Porn." *New York Magazine*, January 26, 2006. https://nymag.com/movies/features/15622/.

Final Destination 3. Directed by James Wong, written by James Wong and Glen Morgan. New Line Cinema, 2006.

Finn, Natalie. "Remembering How Moviegoers Got Psyched to 'See Paris Die' in *House of Wax*." *E! News*, May 6, 2020. https://www.eonline.com/news/1148602/remembering-how-moviegoers-got-psyched-to-see-paris-die-in-house-of-wax.

"Franchise: Final Destination." Box Office Mojo. https://www.boxofficemojo.com/franchise/fr3595013893/.

Hobbs, Thomas. "Horror Effects Icon Tom Savini: 'My Work Looks So Authentic Because I've Seen the Real Thing.'" *The Independent*, August 3, 2020. https://www.independent.co.uk/arts-entertainment/films/features/tom-savini-interview-horror-effects-dawn-of-the-dead-friday-the-13th-a9646331.html.

Kerner, Aaron Michael. *Torture Porn in the Wake of 9/11*. Rutgers University Press, 2015.

Levine, Rebecca. *Final Destination: End of the Line*. Black Flame, 2005.

McIntee, David. *Final Destination: Destination Zero*. Black Flame, 2005.

Puar, Jasbir. *The Right to Maim*. Duke University Press, 2017.

Rhodes, Natasha. *Final Destination: Dead Reckoning*. Black Flame, 2005.

Sleepaway Camp. Directed by Robert Hiltzik, written by Robert Hiltzik. American Eagle Films, 1983.

Walker, John. Interview by Joe Galloway. *Witness to War Oral History Project.* C-SPAN, September 21, 2015. https://www.c-span.org/video/?445803-1/john-walker-vietnam-war-oral-history-interview.

Southern Fried

Hansen, Gunnar. *Chain Saw Confidential: How We Made the World's Most Notorious Horror Movie.* Chronicle Books, 2013.

Texas Chain Saw Massacre, The. Directed by Tobe Hooper, written by Tobe Hooper and Kim Henkel. Bryanston Distributing Company, 1974.

Cutting in Miniature

Lizzie. Directed by Craig William Macneill, written by Bryce Kass. Saban Films, 2018.

Monroe, Rachel. *Savage Appetites: Four True Stories of Women, Crime, and Obsession.* Scribner, 2019.

Peterson, M. Jeane, J. Eric Smithburn, and Joyce G. Williams, eds. *Lizzie Borden: A Case Book of Family and Crime in the 1890s.* T.I.S. Publications, 1980.

Yuko, Elizabeth. "Lizzie Borden: Why a 19th-Century Murder Still Fascinates Us." *Rolling Stone,* August 4, 2016. https://www.rollingstone.com/culture/culture-features/lizzie-borden-why-a-19th-century-axe-murder-still-fascinates-us-250467/.

Preliminary Materials for a Theory of the Werewolf Girl

Carter, Angela. *The Bloody Chamber and Other Stories.* Harper and Row, 1979.

"Domestic Box Office for July 12, 2024." Box Office Mojo. https://www.boxofficemojo.com/date/2024-07-12/weekly/.

Ginger Snaps. Directed by John Fawcett, written by Karen Walton. Motion International, 2000.

Longlegs. Directed by Osgood Perkins, written by Osgood Perkins. Neon, 2024.

Priest, Hannah, ed. *She-wolf: A Cultural History of Female Werewolves.* Manchester University Press, 2017.

Wolf Man, The. Directed by George Waggner, written by Curt Siodmak. Universal Pictures, 1941.

REFERENCES

Devotion

Fiedler, Leslie A. "Introduction." In *Waiting for God*, by Simone Weil. Harper Perennial, 2009.

Saint Maud. Directed by Rose Glass, written by Rose Glass. A24, 2019.

Weil, Simone. *Gravity and Grace*, translated by Emma Crawford and Mario von der Ruhr. Routledge, 2002.

Weil, Simone. *Waiting for God*, translated by Emma Craufurd [sic]. G.P. Putnam's Sons, 1951.

Crazy in Love

American Psychiatric Association. "Gender Dysphoria Diagnosis." Psychiatry.org, accessed September 7, 2024. https://www.psychiatry.org/psychiatrists/diversity/education/transgender-and-gender-nonconforming-patients/gender-dysphoria-diagnosis.

Antichrist. Directed by Lars von Trier, written by Lars von Trier. Zentropa, 2009.

Febos, Melissa. *Abandon Me: Memoirs*. Bloomsbury USA, 2018.

Price, Devon. *Unmasking Autism: Discovering the New Faces of Neurodiversity*. Penguin Random House, 2022.

Secretary. Directed by Steven Shainberg, written by Erin Cressida Wilson, based on the story by Mary Gaitskill. Lionsgate Films, 2002.

Washuta, Elissa. *White Magic*. Tin House Books, 2021.

Weil, Simone. *Gravity and Grace*, translated by Emma Crawford and Mario von der Ruhr. Routledge, 2002.

Zambreno, Kate. *Heroines*. Semiotext(e), 2012.

Uncanny Valley of the Dolls

Note: The majority of these sources—including newspaper clippings—were sourced from the Greer Lankton Archives at the Mattress Factory, accessible in person and online at lankton.mattress.org. A more thorough list of sources follows.

Avgikos, Jan. *Artforum* review of Lankton's work [n.d.].

Cotter, Holland. "Greer Lankton." *Arts Magazine*, November 1984.

REFERENCES

Goldin, Nan. "A Rebel Whose Dolls Embodied Her Demons." *New York Times*, December 22, 1996.

Goldin, Nan. Letter to Greer. June 24, 1992.

Goldin, Nan. *The Other Side, 1972–1992*. Steidl, 2019 (Reissue).

"Heterogeneous: An Exhibit by Gay, Lesbian, Bisexual, and Transgender Artists," February 20–March 8, 1996. Katherine E. Nash Gallery, University of Minnesota.

"Interview with Greer Lankton." *i-D*, 1985.

Indiana, Gary. "Greer Lankton at Civilian Warfare." *Art in America*, November 1984.

Jojo Baby. Personal interview, conducted August 2022.

Karuza, Karen. Personal interview, conducted August 2022.

Karuza, Karen. *Through the Eyes of a Doll: Greer Lankton and the Body of Sex and Gender Identity*. Unpublished thesis, 2007.

Kroll, Eric. *Greer Lankton Surrounded by Her Sculptures*. Photograph, 1984.

Lankton, Bill and Lynn. Death announcement draft, 1996.

Lankton, Greer and Joyce Randall Senechal. "The Contortionist." Short film, 1978. https://www.youtube.com/watch?v=aMXbJCEZtAo.

Lankton, Greer. Daily planners and journals, 1980–1988.

Lankton, Greer. Doubled photograph in hospital bed, n.d.

Lankton, Greer. Letter to Jan, June 3, 1992.

Lankton, Greer. List of Strengths, 1991.

Lankton, Greer. *Operation Day*. Watercolor, 1981.

Lankton, Greer. *Sketchbook, September 1977*. Primary Information, 2023.

Lankton, Greer. *The Story of Greg's Teeth*. Drawing, April 27, 1972.

Lida, Marc. "Dollmaker Greer Makes Ambiguous Creations." *The West Side Spirit*, January 24, 1988.

McCormick, Carlo. "My Life Is Art: An Interview with Greer Lankton." *East Village Eye*, v.5 no.45 (Nov 1984).

Monroe, Paul and Andrew Durbin. "Unalterable Strangeness." *Flash Art*, April 30, 2015. https://web.archive.org/web/20191120092634/https://flash-art.com/article/unalterable-strangeness/.

Mori, Masahiro. "The Uncanny Valley." Translated by Karl F. MacDorman and Norri Kageki. *IEEE Spectrum*, June 12, 2012. https://spectrum.ieee.org/the-uncanny-valley.

Newcomb, David. Personal interview, conducted October 3, 2022.

Randall Senechal, Joyce. *Our Time*. 2004.

Rilke, Rainer Maria. "The Unfortunate Fate of Childhood Dolls." Translated by Idris Parry, 1994. 1913. Republished in The Paris Review, 25 May 2015. https://www.theparisreview.org/blog/2018/05/25/the-unfortunate-fate-of-childhood-dolls/.

Rohr, Lawrence P. Letter referring to Greer's relapse and subsequent treatment, January 15, 1991. Counseling Innovations, Glenwood, IL.

Smith, Roberta. "Greer Lankton, 38, A Sculptor Who Turned Dolls into Fantasy." *New York Times*, November 25, 1996.

The Mattress Factory. "Greer Lankton—It's all about ME, Not You." YouTube Video, October 6, 2009. https://www.youtube.com/watch?v=v_73q7NwS7o.

Thom, Kai Cheng. "Where Did She Go? A Trans Girl Ghost Story." In *I Hope We Choose Love: A Trans Girl's Notes from the End of the World*. Arsenal Pulp Press, 2018.

Thomas, Mary. "Artist's Power Lingers Even After Death." *Pittsburgh Post-Gazette*, November 30, 1996.

Vendelin, Carmen. "Sex, Gender, and the Body of the Dollmaker: Carmen Vendelin Talks to Greer Lankton." 1995.

Winakor, Bess. "Art Institute Alumni Exhibit Opening Even Has a Living Doll." *Chicago Sun-Times*, October 7, 1976.

Postlude

Fragkaki, Iro, et al. "Reduced Freezing in Posttraumatic Stress Disorder Patients While Watching Affective Pictures." *Frontiers in Psychiatry 8*, no. 39 (2017). https://www.ncbi.nlm.nih.gov/pmc/articles/PMC5348645/.

About the Author

ZEFYR LISOWSKI is a trans and queer writer, artist, and North Carolinian living in New York City. A 2023 NYSCA/NYFA Fellow and 2023 Queer|Art Fellow, she's the author of the poetry collections *Girl Work*, winner of the 2022 Noemi Book Prize, and *Blood Box*, winner of the Black River Editor's Choice Award from Black Lawrence Press. From 2016 to 2024, she served as poetry coeditor for the Whiting Award–winning *Apogee Journal*. She's seen grave robbers twice. Visit her at zefyrlisowski.com.